MW00414113

Standoff

STANDOFF

Why Reconciliation Fails Indigenous People and How to Fix It

Bruce McIvor

NIGHTWOOD EDITIONS

2021

Copyright © Bruce McIvor, 2021

2 3 4 5 6 — 26 25 24 23 22

ALL RIGHTS RESERVED. No part of this publication may be reproduced, stored in a retrieval system or transmitted, in any form or by any means, without prior permission of the publisher or, in the case of photocopying or other reprographic copying, a licence from Access Copyright, the Canadian Copyright Licensing Agency, www.accesscopyright.ca, info@accesscopyright.ca.

Nightwood Editions
P.O. Box 1779
Gibsons, BC V0N 1V0
Canada
www.nightwoodeditions.com

COVER DESIGN: TopShelf Creative
TYPOGRAPHY: Carleton Wilson

  Canada Council Conseil des Arts
for the Arts du Canada

 BRITISH COLUMBIA ARTS COUNCIL BRITISH COLUMBIA

Nightwood Editions acknowledges the support of the Canada Council for the Arts, the Government of Canada, and the Province of British Columbia through the BC Arts Council.

This book has been produced on 100% post-consumer recycled, ancient-forest-free paper, processed chlorine-free and printed with vegetable-based dyes.

Printed and bound in Canada.

LIBRARY AND ARCHIVES CANADA CATALOGUING IN PUBLICATION

Title: Standoff : why reconciliation fails Indigenous people and how to fix it / Bruce McIvor.
Names: McIvor, Bruce, author.
Description: Includes bibliographical references and index.
Identifiers: Canadiana (print) 20210271701 | Canadiana (ebook) 20210273763 | ISBN 9780889714205 (softcover) | ISBN 9780889714212 (HTML)
Subjects: LCSH: Indigenous peoples—Canada—Social conditions. | LCSH: Indigenous peoples—Canada—Government relations. | LCSH: Indigenous peoples—Legal status, laws, etc.—Canada. | LCSH: Indigenous peoples—Canada—Public opinion.| LCSH: Canada—Race relations. | LCSH: Canada—Ethnic relations. | LCSH: Reconciliation.
Classification: LCC E78.C2 M35 2021 | DDC 305.897/071—dc23

This book is dedicated to Emilie whose strength, support and clarity of vision have inspired me to imagine a better world and to play my small part in making it a reality, one step at a time.

Table of Contents

Preface

Not long after I became a lawyer, I found myself one sunny day in a standoff on the edge of the Thompson River in Nlaka'pamux territory in the interior of British Columbia. Two clients and I were toe to toe with three government officials. No one spoke. The only sounds were the rushing water of the river in freshet and a woodpecker's hammering on a nearby tree.

While the anger and frustration engulfing our small group was palpable, stronger still was my clients' resolve. It was their land. It was their responsibility to care for the river, the fish, the birds and the plants. Regardless of what happened in that moment, they would not concede, they would not back down.

Writing the essays in this book has been my attempt to use the development of the law around Indigenous rights in Canada over the last ten years to capture that moment in time, to help explain the legal and historical forces that created it and, hopefully, to suggest a way forward based on honesty and respect. Although all the essays are grounded in my knowledge of Canadian constitutional law and Canadian history, they are written for non-lawyers. Most began as opinion pieces and case comments I shared with clients, colleagues and a wider audience across Canada and around the world.

When I set out to put together this collection, I considered rewriting many of these essays with the benefit of hindsight. But I quickly realized this would deprive them of their value. By respecting their historical embeddedness and adding short addendums where helpful, I hope these essays capture how the development of Canadian Aboriginal law over the last ten years has simultaneously supported and thwarted the recognition of Indigenous rights and legal orders.

I have always believed there is much more to being an Indigenous rights lawyer than arguing cases in court. Being part of the national dialogue is just as important. This collection is my contribution to that dialogue. I hope all readers, Indigenous and non-Indigenous, find in it a moment that resonates with their personal history, with their values and aspirations, with their conscience and responsibilities. The possibility of resolving the standoff is born in that moment.

Acknowledgements

Professionally, I am nothing without my clients. Whatever value there is in this book is primarily due to their visions, teachings and patience. The entire team at First Peoples Law has been instrumental in bringing this work to publication. I am especially indebted to my colleagues Kate Gunn and Cody O'Neil. Cody's comments and editing skills improved many of these essays. He has an outstanding future in the law ahead of him. Kate helped me develop many of the essays, added valuable insights and corrected my mistakes. Kate is a top-notch lawyer, trusted colleague and dedicated advocate for Indigenous Peoples.

Residential Schools and Reconciliation: A Canada Day Proposal

News of 215 Indigenous children buried on the grounds of the Kamloops Indian Residential School has shocked Canada and the world. Canadians are calling for real change in the country's relationship with Indigenous Peoples. Apologies are not enough. The federal government must take a meaningful step toward dismantling the existing structures of systemic racism that led to the death of the 215 children and hundreds of other Indigenous children across the country. One such step would be for the federal government to repudiate the Doctrine of Discovery.

The Doctrine of Discovery

The Doctrine of Discovery is the Western legal principle that European countries extinguished Indigenous sovereignty and acquired the underlying title to Indigenous Peoples' lands upon "discovering" them. The principle derives from an 1820s decision of the US Supreme Court. An early champion of the principle was US President Andrew Jackson, infamous for signing into law the Indian Removal Act of 1830.

The Doctrine of Discovery entered Canadian law in the 1880s through the *St. Catherine's Milling* decision, the first major court decision to address the nature of Indigenous land rights in Canada. When the Supreme Court of Canada began its modern consideration of Indigenous rights in the late twentieth century, it relied on the doctrine to explain how colonizing European countries gained the underlying title to Indigenous lands.

Despite the appeals of intervenors in the 2014 *Tsilhqot'in* decision, the Supreme Court refused to abandon the Doctrine of Discovery. Instead, the court perpetuated and reinforced the racist, dehumanizing and indefensible principle that with a sleight of hand the British Crown acquired the underlying title to Indigenous lands through a simple assertion of sovereignty. The Truth and Reconciliation Commission denounced the Doctrine of Discovery. Four of the commission's calls to action (45, 46, 47 and 49) urge governments and religious denominations to publicly disavow it—Canadian governments have responded with silence.

A Long Shadow

The doctrine is not simply a historical or legal curiosity—it informs every aspect of federal and provincial governments' relationships with Indigenous Peoples.

The Supreme Court of Canada has repeatedly stated that at its heart reconciliation is about reconciling the pre-existing rights of Indigenous Peoples with the assertion of Crown sovereignty. The phrase "assertion of Crown sovereignty" is a Canadian euphemism for the Doctrine of Discovery. Every time Canadians read in the news about "reconciliation" they are entering a national conversation based on the racist and dehumanizing Doctrine of Discovery.

When Canadian governments consider making a decision with the potential to affect Indigenous rights protected under section 35 of the constitution they must consult and accommodate Indigenous Peoples. The duty to consult is based on Canadian governments' claim to the underlying title to Indigenous lands. Every time governments across the country engage in consultation with First Nations they invoke the Doctrine of Discovery.

Even when Indigenous Peoples succeed in establishing Aboriginal title to their lands, they cannot escape the Doctrine of Discovery. In Canadian law, Indigenous rights protected under section 35 of the constitution, including Aboriginal title, are not absolute. Where justified, provincial and federal governments can infringe Aboriginal title in the name of reconciliation.

The Supreme Court has suggested that Aboriginal title might be infringed for a wide range of purposes including the development of agriculture, forestry, mining and hydroelectric power, as well as the building of infrastructure and the settlement of foreign populations. The Doctrine of Discovery is the back door through which Canadian governments can override Aboriginal title.

The long, insidious reach of the Doctrine of Discovery extends beyond the courts and government interactions with Indigenous people. Canadian private property rights are based on the Doctrine of Discovery. Every time Canadians sell a house and rub their hands with glee at the wealth their property has generated, they are complicit in perpetuating the Doctrine of Discovery.

Repudiate the Doctrine of Discovery

Much has been made of the federal government's proposed legislation to implement the United Nations Declaration on the Rights of Indigenous Peoples (UNDRIP). I have my doubts about its likely impact (see "A Cold Rain Falls" on page 174). Even if the legislation is passed into law, it will not change Canadian law's reliance on the Doctrine of Discovery.

It has become clear that Canadians cannot expect Canadian courts to rectify this injustice. Rather than denounce the Doctrine of Discovery, the Supreme Court of Canada has relied on it to build the framework for its interpretation of Indigenous rights protected under the constitution. It has done so because acknowledging the legal and moral illegitimacy of the Doctrine of Discovery would raise questions about the court's authority over Indigenous people and Indigenous lands.

There is a direct correlation between the death of the 215 Indigenous children at the Kamloops Indian Residential School and the Doctrine of Discovery. The residential school system was founded on denial—the denial of Indigenous Peoples' human rights, the denial of Indigenous sovereignty, the denial of Indigenous land rights. Even in death, the 215 children could not escape the Doctrine of Discovery—the Canadian state took their lives and claimed the very land they were buried in.

Reconciliation has become a four-letter word for many Indigenous people not simply because of a continuous stream of empty and broken promises. Reconciliation fails Indigenous people, and all of Canada, because it rests on a legal house of cards—the morally reprehensible Doctrine of Discovery. By finally and officially rejecting the doctrine, Canada will be able to enter a relationship of respect and coexistence with Indigenous Peoples—respect for Indigenous Peoples' inherent rights and right to protect their land and their children.

With the Supreme Court of Canada unwilling to act, the responsibility rests on the Canadian Parliament. To honour the 215 children and to set the country on a path to true reconciliation, on Canada Day, July 1, 2021, the Prime Minister should have announced that his government would introduce legislation to repudiate the Doctrine of Discovery.

Negotiate or Litigate?

While Indigenous Peoples across Canada vary widely in their challenges and opportunities, they all have two fundamental objectives in common: to benefit from and exercise jurisdiction over their lands.

With governments often unwilling to address First Nations' real concerns, achieving these objectives increasingly depends on making agreements with industry to share benefits from development and to participate in ongoing decision-making about how these developments will proceed.

Certain proposed developments are simply beyond the pale and the affected First Nation will never consent to them proceeding, regardless of what benefits and decision-making powers are on offer. More often a First Nation will be open to discussing how and on what terms a proposed development might proceed in its territory.

Typically, a First Nation reviews the project with community members and hires consultants to advise on the environmental, social and economic impacts of a proposed development. At the same time, they work on negotiating the best agreement possible with government or the company (or both), one that includes not just financial benefits but also many other provisions including processes for environmental monitoring and protection.

If negotiations are successful, leadership takes the tentative agreement and all the other information that has been gathered to the community. They explain how the project is likely to negatively affect the First Nation and its lands, how it will hopefully benefit current and future generations and how the First Nation will be involved in its ongoing operation. It is then up to the community to decide whether or not to give its consent for the project to proceed.

But sometimes First Nations, government and industry are unable to reach a negotiated agreement. That's when the question arises for many First Nations: Negotiate or litigate?

The decision to litigate is most often made because government has failed to meet its obligations to respect Aboriginal title, rights and treaty rights and the First Nation and the company cannot agree on how to resolve the issues between themselves. First Nations are left with few options. They either grit their teeth and continue to accept the status quo or a subpar agreement, or they go to court.

As much as war analogies proliferate in litigation circles, they are rarely applicable when a First Nation files a lawsuit. This is because even when they win a legal battle, First Nations are not simply handed solutions by the court—as I often explain to my clients, judges are not Santa Claus.

At best, and especially when First Nations are seeking to enforce their Aboriginal title, rights or treaty rights, the courts will make orders or declarations that will hopefully set the table for negotiated agreements with either government or industry, but they do not mandate an agreement or its terms. For First Nations success in court usually leads to more negotiations.

Ironically, it's not just successful court challenges that result in negotiated settlements. When a First Nation loses at the first level of court, it often appeals. Before the appeal is heard, government and/or the company often reach a negotiated settlement with the First Nation and the appeal is dropped. This can happen for a variety of reasons.

First, government and the company might worry that the appeal judges will disagree with the lower court's decision. It might be better to reach a settlement and avoid the possibility of a First Nation win on appeal that sets a wider precedent.

Second, even though the First Nation lost the first round, by pursuing the case to court and then filing an appeal, it has demonstrated it is in the fight for the long haul. Some governments and many companies decide they do not want the negatives that come with drawn-out litigation, including uncertainty around permits, difficulty raising capital and delays in construction.

The reality is that negotiation and litigation are not mutually exclusive. While most First Nations prefer a negotiated agreement based on their consent to a project that will affect their Aboriginal title, rights and treaty rights, they also realize that government and industry might simply have a different understanding of what is required.

If the government response is unsatisfactory and it reaches an impasse with the company, a First Nation hopefully has access to other options to defend its constitutional rights. Litigation is often the last recourse to achieving successful negotiations.

Who Are the "aboriginal peoples of Canada"?

In the spring of 1811, a party of four Hudson's Bay Company employees led by David Thompson slid a roughly made cedar canoe into the most northern tributary of the Columbia River and drifted southward in search of the Pacific Ocean. After two months of travelling, they met a group of nsyilxcen-speaking Indigenous people at Kettle Falls in current-day Washington State. Thompson reached the mouth of the Columbia later that summer and then retraced his steps upriver, where he again encountered nsyilxcen-speaking Indigenous people north of Kettle Falls near current-day Revelstoke, British Columbia.

One hundred and ninety-nine years later and eighty kilometres north of Kettle Falls, on the Canadian side of the Canada–US border, Rick Desautel shot an elk. Desautel is an American citizen and a member of the Lakes Tribe of the Confederated Tribes of the Colville Reservation. After informing local conservation officers of his success, Desautel was charged with hunting without a licence and hunting big game while not being a resident of British Columbia. Desautel's defence was that he had a right to hunt protected under section 35(1) of the Canadian constitution because he was a descendant of the Indigenous people Thompson met in 1811 on the upper Columbia River.

For ten years the case worked its way through the Canadian courts, with Desautel winning at every level. In fall 2020 it reached the Supreme Court of Canada. There the court was called on to decide whether or not an Indigenous group whose members are neither Canadian citizens nor residents of Canada can be included in the "aboriginal peoples of Canada" within the meaning of section 35(1) of the Canadian constitution.

The court concluded the reference to "aboriginal peoples of Canada" in the Canadian constitution means the modern-day successors of Indigenous societies who, at the time of contact with Europeans, occupied lands that later became part of "Canada." The court held that Desautel had been exercising an Aboriginal right protected under section 35 of the Canadian constitution despite being an American citizen, because the Lakes Tribe was a modern-day successor group of the nsyilxcen-speaking Indigenous people Thompson encountered in 1811.

The court explained that modern-day successor groups located outside Canada are part of the "aboriginal peoples of Canada" because to exclude them would repudiate the purpose of section 35 of the constitution: the recognition of Indigenous Peoples' occupation of their lands prior to the arrival of Europeans and the necessity of reconciling this fact with the assertion of Crown sovereignty.

To facilitate this clarification on who the "aboriginal peoples of Canada" are, the court created a new threshold requirement for Aboriginal rights claims. Before considering the question of whether an Aboriginal right exists, a court must satisfy itself that the Indigenous group claiming the right is part of the "aboriginal peoples of Canada." In most cases, this threshold question will not arise because the answer is obvious, like in the case of a First Nation whose members are Canadian citizens.

If there is uncertainty as to whether an Indigenous group is a modern-day successor of Indigenous people who occupied lands that later became part of Canada, the court identified factors to be considered by lower courts in making a determination, including the following:

- Did the historical Indigenous collective split over time?
- Did two groups merge into one?
- Is there evidence of a shared ancestry, language, culture, laws, political institutions and territory?

Importantly, while the court confirmed the trial judge's finding that the Lakes Tribe was a successor group to the nsyilxcen-speaking Indigenous people encountered by David Thompson, the court reiterated there may be other Indigenous modern-day successor groups. In Canada, nsyilxcen is the language of the *Syilx* Okanagan Nation. Many *Syilx* Okanagan Nation members trace their ancestry to the Indigenous people Thompson met on the upper Columbia River in 1811.

The court emphasized that under Canadian law, Indigenous groups located outside Canada who are part of the "aboriginal peoples of Canada" may not necessarily be on an equal footing with Indigenous groups located within Canada. In the context of the duty to consult and accommodate, if there have been no historical interactions with an American group that would have given the Crown knowledge of their claim, there is no free-standing duty to seek them out to give them notice. Similarly, the scope of the duty to consult owed

Indigenous groups outside Canada may differ from what is owed Indigenous groups within Canada.

The Crown may also have to discuss with Indigenous groups located within Canada how they should consult with Indigenous groups outside Canada. Importantly, the court reiterated that ultimately it is up to Indigenous Peoples to define themselves and decide how to make decisions according to their own laws, customs and practices.

The court left many questions unanswered. For example, it did not decide whether an American citizen who is not a resident of Canada has the right to cross the international border to exercise a constitutionally protected right. The court was silent on other issues as well, including on how the new threshold requirement might be modified in the case of rights claimed by the Métis and what the decision means for a possible Aboriginal title claim by an Indigenous group residing outside of Canada. The court declined to address these issues because they did not arise from the facts of the case and because a case based on an individual's defence to charges laid by the Crown is ill-suited for the determination of complex legal issues affecting an entire Indigenous collective.

Why It Matters

Indigenous Peoples with lands and families along both sides of the Canada–US border continue to exist despite the bifurcation of their territories by the international boundary and the devastating effect colonization has had on their lands, languages, laws, cultures, political systems and families. They have survived.

Decolonization is a messy business—that's why it is a road, not a moment in time. The assertion of Crown sovereignty, rooted in the discredited Doctrine of Discovery, puts the heavy burden of reconciliation on the Crown. Instead of shouldering this responsibility, British Columbia and other provinces participating in the *Desautel* appeal relied on the insidious effects of the imposition of the international boundary—the ultimate expression of colonization—to argue that they should not now have to help resolve the messy, unjust history and current reality of colonization. Fortunately, the Supreme Court affirmed section 35 as a bulwark against the ultimate success of colonization. It upheld the promise of section 35 and refused to become the instrument of completing Canada's colonization project.

Indigenous Identity and Canadian Law:
A Personal Journey

The Canadian colonial project intertwines Indigenous identity with the development of Aboriginal law. Oppression and reconciliation partner to classify, legitimize and delegitimize Indigenous people. For every Indigenous person the law intrudes on, whether they see themselves as part of the "Indian, Inuit and Métis peoples of Canada" under section 35 of the constitution, as status or non-status, as "on-reserve" or "off-reserve," this will shape and at times distort their sense of self. The complex relationship between Canadian law and Indigenous identity is difficult to explain or appreciate in the abstract. As with any powerful historical force, at its core colonialism is personal.

This is my story.

With no memories of my father, who died when I was five, my role models growing up were strong, self-reliant women—mother, sisters and grandmother. I saw myself as a take-no-crap farm kid whose parents received phone calls from the local minor hockey league threatening to banish him for fighting and who memorized Shakespeare while picking rocks. My understanding of my family's past was based on snippets of conversations heard around the kitchen table. Slowly I came to understand that we had used to live in the bush north of the Peguis First Nation reserve. At this point we lived a mile south of the reserve, doing our best to farm scattered bits of land on Manitoba's agricultural fringe.

In hindsight, I did many things as a kid that would now be classified as traditional practices: hunting (sweet tea over an open fire), trapping (rows of little pelts hung to dry in my mum's basement), snaring rabbits (my brothers' patience with my clumsy fingers), picking saskatoons (poplar trees singing in the wind above us). These were activities without history—it was what we did, not who we were.

Three incidents complicated my self-identity. The first was a family reunion. My oldest sister, whose energy and optimism are my lodestar, threw herself into researching our family history. The most memorable part of the reunion was the intergenerational jalopy race around hay bales in the field behind my mum's house, but the family tree my sister produced had a more lasting effect. My mother's side softened my resentment for being raised Roman Catholic. Church records allowed my sister to trace my mother's family back to two of the earliest French families to arrive in Acadia and New France in the 1630s. My sister had given me a direct, personal relationship with the Acadian Expulsion, the Plains of Abraham and many other famous and infamous events in early Canadian history.

Her research on my father's side revealed a personal connection with less well understood aspects of Canada's past. My father was descended from Indigenous women (Anishinaabe and Cree) and men who had worked for the Northwest Company and the Hudson's Bay Company (mostly Scots, with the odd Englishman and French Canadian thrown in).

Eventually, they had settled at Red River in what was to become Manitoba.

Initially I was drawn to the men's names on my family tree that I was familiar with from Canadian history. Those such as James Curtis Bird and John Thomas were immortalized with entries in the *Dictionary of Canadian Biography*, the ultimate confirmation of historical significance. But these men soon lost their grip on my imagination, their places filled by the Indigenous women from my family's past, some with names—Mary Oo-menahomisk, Louise Serpente, Elizabeth Montour, Robina Hay—and many without, whose histories, dreams and accomplishments had disappeared from the record like dry leaves on an autumn wind. Who were these silent ancestors whose stories had been lost to me? In what way was I their descendant? What were my obligations to them?

The second incident was applying for law school. In filling out the form I faced the choice of applying in the general category, the Aboriginal category or both. With a decent grade point average, good LSAT score and a PhD in history, I was confident I would be accepted. Importantly, I did not want to take a space from those I thought of as truly Aboriginal, so I only ticked the box for the general category. Then the law school phoned. They had noticed a reference to my Indigenous ancestry in my application and wanted to know if they could slot me in as an Aboriginal student. Again, my family tree swayed to and fro—Mary Oo-menahomisk, Louise Serpente, Elizabeth Montour, Robina Hay—would saying no deny my connection to them? After confirming I was not taking a place from anyone, I agreed. It was one of the most important decisions I have made.

Being part of the Indigenous student body at law school threw me in with the most welcoming, supportive and encouraging group of fellow students I had ever known. Again mostly women, they accepted me as an Indigenous person and inspired me to strive to be a useful part of a struggle both personal and historical; a struggle that predates us, is bigger than us and will outlive us. My nascent Indigenous identity coalesced into an ambition to make a meaningful contribution.

The third incident has been the development of the law on Métis rights, especially the three most important decisions to date from the Supreme Court of Canada: *Powley*, *Manitoba Métis Federation* and *Daniels*. The *Powley* decision, which established the test for Métis rights under section 35 of the constitution, was a watershed moment for the Métis. The courage, fortitude and skill of those who contributed to the ultimate success at the Supreme Court must be acknowledged and appreciated.

But Supreme Court cases are rarely simply about winning and losing. The three-part "Powley test" (ancestry, self-identity and community acceptance) is an example of how long-held government policies of denial force Indigenous people into the courts for recognition. Once there, they become entangled in the history, principles, objectives and compromises of Canada's legal system. At the Supreme Court, non-Indigenous judges with an eye to policy implications and "workability," create legal tests that define and distort Indigenous identity. *Powley* constitutes the Supreme Court's foray into making and unmaking the Métis.

The Supreme Court's *Manitoba Métis Federation* decision also poses significant challenges for the Métis, but at a personal level it underscores the power and significance of the court's moral authority. After over one hundred years of government denial, the court confirmed that a terrible wrong was done to the Red River Métis in the government's failure to fulfill the promises made to them when Manitoba entered Confederation in 1870.

Once again ancestors' names swirled around me—Ann McLennan, James Muir, Isabella Bird—ancestors whose scrip had failed to secure for them, as it had failed hundreds of other Métis children, the rich farmland at Red River that would have bound together the Métis through time and space. While reading the decision I repeatedly paused to think of their children and grandchildren, Colin and Isabella, my grandparents, who were denied their inheritance at Red River and who followed the displaced Peguis First Nation north hoping to carve out a new future between the rocks and swamps of Manitoba's Interlake region.

It was just before seven a.m. on the west coast on April 14, 2016 when I first read the Supreme Court's decision in *Daniels* by which it confirmed the federal government's jurisdiction over the Métis and non-status Indians. The house was quiet, my family was asleep, including my baby girl leaning against my chest. I understood *Daniels* as a significant victory for the Métis and the potential importance of the decision for the thousands of Métis denied services and programs due to the jurisdictional dispute between the federal and provincial governments. Although I did not need these programs and services at the time, I knew that thousands of modern-day Métis did. And I knew they would have benefited my family when my father died and my mum moved us all into an abandoned schoolhouse and scrambled to provide for eight children.

Daniels closed my personal circle on Indigenous identity and Aboriginal law. It brought home how Canadian law, yesterday and today, circumscribes and oppresses Indigenous people through marginalization and validation. Because of my Indigenous ancestry, based on *Daniels* I'm an "Indian" under section 91(24) of the constitution. But that legal, constitutional classification obfuscates more than it illuminates. My life experience is qualitatively different from that of my family members, friends, colleagues and clients who are status or non-status. Lumping us all together as "Indian" (or Aboriginal or Indigenous) dishonours the diversity of lived experiences and smooths over Canada's history of racism and oppression.

Under *Powley* and section 35 of the constitution, I might be able to make a case for being Métis. I meet the first part of the *Powley* test because I self-identify. My self-identification is not based on wearing a sash or speaking Michif. It is because if I did not self-identify as Métis I would be denying my ancestors. Their distinctive dreams and accomplishments would slip closer to oblivion. I would have failed to fulfill my obligations to them. I would dishonour them and myself. I am unprepared to take that final step in the march of colonialism, so I am Métis.

But under Canadian law, self-identification is only the first part of the test for being Métis. I and tens of thousands of other Canadians can and do meet this requirement. To be Métis under the constitution I must trace my Indigenous ancestry back in time to a specific historical Métis community.

This aspect of the *Powley* test is too often lost on individuals who claim to be Métis under section 35 of the constitution. Being descended from the Red River Métis, I would probably meet this second part of the *Powley* test, but I would still have to establish acceptance by the modern-day Red River Métis community.

How do I do this? Although my mother and some of my siblings have migrated back to Red River, I live over one thousand miles away in Vancouver. What if, for whatever reason, I do not want to be a member of a modern Métis organization? Why should a modern political organization be the gatekeeper to my, or anyone else's, rights and identity? If I did decide to apply to join a Métis organization, which one? Who decides on the rules for membership and oversees their application? If I wanted to join, would I be accepted?

My concern was, and continues to be, that through *Powley* the Supreme Court unknowingly sanctioned a replication of the worst aspects of the registration provisions of the Indian Act, but this time with Indigenous people bestowing and denying status. Because I have not joined a Métis organization I would likely fail the *Powley* test—in the eyes of Canadian law I am not Métis. If I did apply and was accepted into an organization purporting to represent the Red River Métis, maybe the Manitoba Métis Federation, would that mean I am Métis under section 35 of the constitution? Maybe not.

An aspect of *Powley* that has trailed me like a brooding cloud, is the court's caution that Métis identity cannot be of "recent vintage." The court's caution neutralizes its repeated recognition that colonialism has disrupted and vilified Indigenous communities. It ignores the court's role in shaping and legitimizing Indigenous identity. In *Powley* the court held out the promise of a port of shelter for thousands of Métis scattered on the sea of colonialism. Its caution against recognizing Métis whose self-identification is of "recent vintage" has driven many Métis back out to sea, afraid of being labelled opportunists.

Through the workings of Canadian law, the Red River Métis diaspora lost their land. Many, especially those with French ancestry, managed to maintain their sense of community, family and history. Others, such as my family, lost their community, their ancestors and their pride in where they came from and who they were. They were left to remake themselves without a past. It left me as a child with a ninety-five-year-old grandmother, born at St. Peter's Parish on the Red River, living out her final days over one hundred fifty kilometres away in my aunt's back room, silent as her grandchildren combed her long, grey hair.

Today Canadian law leaves me uncertain of how to explain to my children who they are. *Daniels, Powley* and *Manitoba Métis Federation* do not define me or mine. Without the voice, the words, the stories of my ancestors, I am silent.

In 2020 I reluctantly made the decision to become a member of the Manitoba Métis Federation. I joined for two reasons. First, having my Manitoba Métis Federation citizenship immunizes me from being unfairly lumped in with "pretendians" who falsely claim to be Indigenous and who have caused much pain and loss. Second, and most importantly, I did it for my kids. I realized that an integral part of healing colonialism's wounds is giving them the space and confidence to speak for themselves.

A New Legal Remedy for Indigenous People

The Supreme Court of Canada's decision in *Manitoba Métis Federation v. Canada* (2013) is a classic example of the court going off in its own direction instead of following the parties' specific arguments. As a result, we now have a new legal remedy available to all Indigenous people seeking to enforce the Crown's constitutional obligations. How effective this new remedy will be in providing justice is an open question.

The case raised numerous historical and legal issues surrounding Canada's promise in 1870 to set aside lands for the Métis at Red River. The main issue was a consideration of section 31 of the 1870 Manitoba Act through which Canada, as part of "the extinguishment of the Indian Title" in Manitoba, agreed to set aside 1,400,000 acres of land to be divided among Métis children. The long history of injustice that followed Canada's failure to fulfill its promise has been at the centre of Métis consciousness for over one hundred fifty years.

At the heart of the Métis legal challenge was the question of what standard of conduct was required of the federal government in its fulfillment of the promise made to the Métis to set aside lands. The Métis argued that Canada had assumed the duties of a fiduciary, meaning it was obligated to act in their best interests, not simply consider the wider public interest, that it had to avoid all conflicts of interest and account for how their land had been administered. In 2010 the Manitoba Court of Appeal held that, among other things, even if Canada did owe a fiduciary duty to the Métis based on section 31, the duty was not breached, and that any claim for breach of a fiduciary duty was now barred by statutory limitations and the Métis' delay in bringing their claim.

The Supreme Court rejected the Métis' argument that Canada breached a fiduciary duty to the Métis children based on section 31 of the Manitoba Act. As part of its reasons on this question, the court held that the Manitoba Métis likely could not make a claim for Aboriginal title because the Métis held land individually, not communally, and they had historically been willing to sell their individual interests to others. Both these facts, according to the court, were contrary to the meaning of Aboriginal title.

But the court did not stop there. Instead it ultimately found for the Métis based on an argument none of the parties had made. The court held that Canada had failed to act honourably in fulfilling its constitutional promise to provide lands for the Métis children. And, because constitutional obligations to Aboriginal people are solemn promises intended to foster reconciliation, the Métis were entitled to a declaration from the court that Canada had failed to act honourably in providing lands under section 31 of the Manitoba Act.

Finally, the court held that Manitoba and Canada could not rely on procedural arguments to stop the court from issuing a declaration that Canada's conduct was dishonourable. The court concluded that it is the protector of the constitution and when a constitutional promise to Aboriginal people is at stake, it cannot be muzzled by mere legislation.

Why It Matters

After over one hundred years of denial by Canada that it had done any wrong by the Métis, the importance of the highest court in the country calling Canada to account should not be underestimated. The court's decision is a powerful vindication of Métis history and an acknowledgement that the outstanding wrong should be remedied, to the extent that it can, through present-day good faith negotiations.

Of importance to all Indigenous people, the court has solidified the principle of the "honour of the Crown" in Canadian common law and has created a new legal remedy available whenever the Crown fails to act diligently to fulfill the purpose of a constitutional promise to Indigenous people. Canada's ongoing failure to live up to the specific promises embedded in the historical treaties is just one area where First Nations are likely to seek declarations from the courts based on this new remedy.

The unanswerable question is how effective this new type of court declaration will prove. In the case of the Métis, the court obviously expects Canada to enter into negotiations to right the wrong done to them. But the court's declaration does not demand any particular type of resolution. It may be that negotiations, at least in the eyes of the Métis, will prove unsatisfactory.

Ultimately, a court declaration that Canada has failed to act honourably to fulfill a constitutional promise to Indigenous people may prove most valuable on the international stage. Such a declaration, especially if from the Supreme Court, combined with the United Nations Declaration on the Rights of Indigenous Peoples (UNDRIP), may ultimately shame Canada into fulfilling outstanding constitutional obligations to Indigenous people.

Since the 2013 *Manitoba Métis Federation* decision, it has become common practice for Indigenous Peoples to challenge government conduct based on an alleged breach of the honour of the Crown. Courts have been receptive to these arguments because while they provide a strong legal basis for ensuring further negotiations, they do not by themselves result in cancelled projects or government authorizations.

What Does the *Daniels* Decision Mean?

The *Daniels* decision of April 14, 2016 is likely one of the most misunderstood decisions ever released by the Supreme Court of Canada. The case arose due to the ongoing squabble between the federal and provincial governments over responsibility for providing programs and services to the Métis and non-status Indians. The Supreme Court was asked to make three declarations:

- that the Métis and non-status Indians are "Indians" under section 91(24) of the Constitution;
- that the federal government owes a fiduciary duty to the Métis and non-status Indians; and
- that the Métis and non-status Indians have a right to be consulted and negotiated with in good faith by the federal government on a collective basis through representatives of their choice, respecting all rights, interests and needs as Aboriginal peoples.

The first declaration required the court to interpret section 91(24) of the constitution. Sections 91 and 92 of the constitution identify subjects that either the federal government or provincial governments have the exclusive jurisdiction to make laws about. For example, the federal government has the exclusive jurisdiction to make laws about the postal service. On the provincial side of the ledger is the exclusive authority to make laws about the management and sale of public lands.

This doesn't mean that one level of government can't make laws that affect topics under the jurisdiction of the other level of government. They can and often do. What it means is that they can't pass a law that intentionally affects a subject under the exclusive jurisdiction of the other level of government or indirectly affects its core, whatever that might be. This is why the provinces can't pass a law specifically about Indian reserves—Indian reserves are "lands reserved for the Indians" under section 91(24) and therefore only the federal government can pass laws about them.

Importantly, just because a subject matter isn't listed under either section 91 (federal powers) or section 92 (provincial powers) doesn't mean neither level of government can pass a law relating to that subject. By default, the federal government has the legislative authority for any subject not mentioned. This is why the federal government's argument that it couldn't legislate regarding the Métis was always self-serving and disingenuous.

What the Court Said

The court made the first declaration. Based on the findings of fact of the trial judge, the court held that when used in section 91(24) of the constitution, "Indians" was intended to include the Métis and non-status Indians. The court declined to make the second and third declarations. The existence of a fiduciary relationship and the possibility of a duty to consult was already settled law. A declaration of an overarching, non-specific fiduciary duty to the Métis or duty to consult the Métis would have been a significant change in the law.

What the Court Did Not Say

The court did not order the federal government to do anything.

The decision doesn't make Métis and non-status Indians "Indians" under the Indian Act.

The court's declaration does not affect any specific individuals or groups of Métis or non-status Indians. The specifics of who the declaration might apply to is a matter for a future court decision.

The court's decision is not about Métis constitutional rights. These rights are protected under a different section of the constitution (section 35). The test for establishing them was set out in the court's *Powley* decision—the test has not changed.

The decision does not mean provincial laws don't apply to the Métis and non-status Indians. The application of provincial laws is a different question for a different day.

The decision does not obligate the federal government to negotiate treaties with the Métis. This was always and remains a possibility. The argument that the federal government couldn't because of section 91(24) was a red herring.

The decision does not mean the Métis have an additional argument for revenue sharing. Section 91(24) is not about rights or interests. It's about the federal government's exclusive legislative powers.

Why It Matters

Courts aren't in the business of making declarations. They only do so when they believe a declaration will have the practical effect of settling a "live controversy." In this case, the court concluded that granting a declaration assigning constitutional authority to make laws affecting the Métis and non-status Indians to the federal government would have "enormous practical utility" for the two groups who until now had been left to rely on government's noblesse oblige (goodwill).

According to the court, the federal government's and the provinces' disagreement over legislative authority over the Métis and non-status Indians had resulted in the latter groups being deprived of much-needed programs and services. The court acknowledged that its declaration would not force the federal government to pass any laws directly affecting the Métis and non-status Indians. Instead, the court concluded that granting the declaration would create certainty and accountability as to which level of government the Métis and non-status Indians should turn to for policies to address their historical disadvantages—they should turn to the federal government.

What does the *Daniels* decision mean? Put simply, the Métis and non-status Indians should look to the federal government in the hopes of negotiating improved programs and services, but there's no legal obligation on the federal government to do anything specific.

Hopefully the decision will lead to better programs and services for the Métis and non-status Indians. If so, it will prove to be an important victory. Personally, the decision leaves me cold. Historically, section 91(24) was understood as a shield—it was intended to stop the provinces from passing laws that directly interfere with "Indians and lands reserved for the Indians." The benefit of the Métis and non-status Indians now being granted this protection is likely a lot less than it once would have been, because in 2014 the Supreme Court in *Tsilhqot'in* and *Grassy Narrows* significantly narrowed the scope of the protection.

In *Daniels*, the court emphasized a different purpose for section 91(24)—the control of Aboriginal people. As the court explained, assigning the Crown's law-making authority to the federal government facilitated Canada's westward expansion, including the development of laws and policies intended to stop Aboriginal people, including the Métis, from resisting non-Indigenous settlement of their lands. Section 91(24) was, and is, an instrument of colonization.

As a Métis person whose ancestors were deprived of their land at Red River, I take no satisfaction in the Supreme Court confirming the federal government's exclusive authority to make laws about me, my children or the Red River Métis. On a broader level, the decision is out of step with the aspirations of most Indigenous Peoples in Canada and around the world. Rather than seeking confirmation of the Crown's jurisdiction over them, Indigenous Peoples are striving to achieve recognition of their own jurisdiction. In the end, I'm left wondering what the Métis who fought and died resisting Canada's exercise of jurisdiction over them would make of the *Daniels* decision.

How to Fulfill the Duty to Consult

As governments, industry and First Nations continue to disagree on what it takes to fulfill the duty to consult, resource development projects stall and public frustration grows. This is despite that for over fifteen years, and culminating in the 2014 *Tsilhqot'in* decision, the courts have established and elaborated on the principles underpinning the duty to consult.

If governments, industry and First Nations are going to trust each other and work together, we need to dispel common misconceptions about the duty to consult, agree on basic requirements and outline a path to reconciliation.

Duty to Consult Is Not Public Consultation

First, the duty to consult is qualitatively different than consultation with the general public. It is a constitutional duty owed solely to Indigenous people. It exists because Indigenous Peoples with their own laws and customs controlled the lands and waters now called Canada before non-Indigenous people arrived. European states bent on colonization recognized that based on their own laws, they could not simply ignore the fact of the original inhabitants—Indigenous and non-Indigenous interests had to be reconciled. The duty to consult is part of this ongoing national project.

Minimum Requirements

While specific obligations vary with the circumstances, the courts have identified minimum requirements for meaningful consultation with First Nations. Consultation must begin at the earliest stages of planning and cannot be postponed. Governments must consult in good faith with an honest intention of substantially addressing Indigenous Peoples' concerns. Government officials must have the required powers to change the project because consultation without the possibility of accommodation is meaningless.

Governments must listen carefully to concerns and work to minimize adverse effects on Aboriginal rights and treaty rights. They should be open to abandoning or rejecting proposals. If there is a decision to proceed, governments should demonstrably integrate responses to Indigenous Peoples' concerns into revised plans of action. If suggestions for changes to a project are rejected, an explanation is required.

As governments love to remind First Nations, there is no Indigenous veto. This is likely the most misunderstood statement surrounding the duty to consult. The implication is that because there is no veto, ultimately governments can do what they want and First Nations cannot stop them. That line of thinking is incompatible with the requirements outlined above. It leads to distrust, frustration and litigation.

Importantly, consultation is not addition. You do not add up the number of meetings and comments to determine whether consultation has been adequate. As former chief justice Lance Finch of the BC Court of Appeal once noted, consultation must be more than an opportunity for Indigenous Peoples to blow off steam.

In sum, consultation requires sufficiently mandated government officials to enter into good faith negotiations with Indigenous Peoples based on flexible proposals, to carefully listen and respond to concerns, and to be open to changing their plans.

Consultation Plus

And then there are the projects that require more than consultation.

The consultation requirements described above apply to First Nations with Aboriginal rights not yet recognized by government. For First Nations with recognized rights, including treaty First Nations, governments may have to do more than consult. They may have to justify any infringement of those rights. This can be thought of as "consultation plus."

When justification is required, in addition to the duty to consult, governments must demonstrate that the project contributes to a compelling and substantial objective consistent with their fiduciary duty to Indigenous Peoples. This is much more than deciding the project is in the public interest. To meet the justification test, governments must demonstrate that the project is designed to minimally affect Aboriginal rights, and that the government's broader public goal in respect of the project advances the overarching objective of reconciliation.

Consent-Based Reconciliation

No one suggests these requirements are not onerous. They should be, considering what is at stake—the overriding of constitutionally protected rights, a protection intended to reconcile newcomers' interests with those of the Indigenous Peoples of Canada.

Of course, there is another path to reconciliation—it is based on consent. Were governments to seriously seek Indigenous Peoples' consent, they would likely find that in many cases there are respectful and mutually beneficial ways forward. Where no such path exists, it's likely that the project could never have been justified in the first place.

The Piecemeal Infringement of Treaty Rights

During the early years of the development of modern Aboriginal law in Canada, First Nations with so-called "numbered treaties" could argue that governments were obligated to justify any infringement of their treaty rights. This changed with the Supreme Court's 2005 *Mikisew* decision. The court held that when governments "take up" land under the numbered treaties (including exploiting Indigenous lands for forestry, mining etc.), their obligations are limited to consultation and perhaps accommodation. Only when a provincial government takes up so much land as to leave a First Nation with no meaningful ability to exercise their treaty rights might they have crossed the line and infringed the treaty.

For many treaty First Nations, this has meant the slow erosion of their treaty rights by a thousand cuts—no one decision fatal by itself, but the cumulative effect devastating nonetheless. Blueberry River First Nations in Treaty 8, for example, estimates that two-thirds of its traditional territory has been developed for industrial purposes or is within 250 metres of industrial development. At the current rate of development, by 2060 all of its lands will have either been developed or be within 250 metres of development.

But Blueberry River decided to fight back. In March 2015 it filed a lawsuit against British Columbia, alleging the

Province had breached Treaty 8 because the cumulative effect of development in its territory (including forestry, mining, hydroelectricity and oil and gas) would soon make it impossible for its members to meaningfully exercise their treaty rights. Following the filing of the lawsuit, Blueberry River sought an injunction to prevent British Columbia from selling fifteen timber sale licences pursuant to forestry plans approved in 2010 and 2011. Blueberry River alleged that the sale of the licences would contribute to the cumulative effects of development in its territory and therefore should not be allowed until its lawsuit for treaty infringement was heard.

The court concluded that the "balance of convenience" did not favour the First Nation and so denied the injunction application. In doing so, the court considered the relationship between the specific logging activities Blueberry River had sought an injunction against and the wider alleged treaty breach, which it characterized as the cumulative effect of numerous developments due to continued unchecked development in the First Nation's territory.

The court emphasized that the area intended for logging under the timber sale licences was less than a tenth of 1 percent of Blueberry River's territory and that about 90 percent of ongoing development complained of by the First Nation would be unaffected by the injunction. It concluded that the proposed logging was not the tipping point beyond which a First Nation might not be able to meaningfully exercise its treaty rights.

A central concern for the court was that if Blueberry River succeeded on the application, there might be a series of applications against discrete development proposals that could effectively put a stop to all development in Blueberry River's territory without its approval. The court left open the possibility that the First Nation might come back to court and obtain a general injunction against all development in its territory, but concluded that the public interest would not be served by a piecemeal, project by project approach to protecting the First Nation's treaty rights.

Subsequently, Blueberry River sought a general injunction that was also denied by the court. Their treaty infringement trial eventually concluded in 2020 and the court's decision was released in early July 2021. In a surprising but welcomed clarification of the law, the court did not accept the argument that the provincial government would only be liable for treaty infringement if it took up so much of Blueberry River's land that First Nation members would no longer be able to meaningfully exercise their treaty rights. Instead, the court held the Province will have infringed the treaty if taking up land significantly infringed the First Nation's treaty rights. Based on this higher standard, the Province was found to have breached Treaty 8 because it had failed to address the cumulative effect of resource development. The Province decided not to appeal the decision and instead entered into negotiations with Blueberry River to ensure the protection of the First Nation's treaty rights.

Why It Matters

The piecemeal limitation of treaty rights is one of the greatest challenges First Nations face in their ongoing struggle to defend their treaty rights. Unfortunately, the tipping point for treaty infringement is in sight for many treaty First Nations. Carry the Kettle Nakoda Nation has filed a similar treaty infringement claim against Saskatchewan and Canada regarding agricultural and industrial development in Treaty 4. Beaver Lake Cree Nation has also filed a treaty infringement lawsuit against Alberta, alleging the cumulative effect of oil and gas development in its territory prevents the meaningful exercise of its treaty rights. The 120-day "Tar Sands Trial" is scheduled to begin in January 2024. The Beaver Lake claim is now the subject of an upcoming appeal at the Supreme Court of Canada on the issues of advanced costs.

The Blueberry River decision gives all treaty First Nations new hope that their legitimate concerns will finally be addressed. To date, governments have refused to seriously consider cumulative effects and support First Nation–driven land use planning. This undermines effective responses to the steady erosion of treaty rights. Governments must recognize that it is in everyone's interests, Indigenous and non-Indigenous alike, to work with First Nations to find real solutions. If not, frustration will grow, lawsuits will be filed, risk will increase and opportunities will be lost.

The Duty to Consult—A Second-Best Alternative

Asserting an Aboriginal right and *proving* an Aboriginal right are very different things and lead to very different legal obligations. Court decisions from the Northwest Territories and Alberta on Métis Aboriginal rights demonstrate the differing legal requirements for asserting versus proving an Aboriginal right and why they are important.

Enge v. Mandeville et al., 2013 NWTSC 33

The size of the Northwest Territories' Bathurst caribou herd plummeted between 2006 and 2009. As an emergency conservation measure, the Tlicho Government and the Government of the Northwest Territories (GNWT) limited the 2010–11 harvest to three hundred caribou divided between the Tlicho and the Yellowknives Dene First Nation. The North Slave Métis Alliance argued that the GNWT had breached its duty to consult and accommodate by not allocating part of the harvest to the Métis.

In its reasons for the decision, the court emphasized that even dubious or weak claims of Aboriginal rights will trigger the duty to consult. Once the duty is triggered, the Crown must prepare a preliminary assessment of how strong the unproven claim is and the potential impact of the pending decision on asserted Aboriginal rights. This assessment, which should be shared with the Aboriginal people claiming the right, guides the scope and content of consultation. The court concluded that the GNWT had breached its obligation to consult with the Métis because even though the Métis had a credible (though as yet unproven) claim to an Aboriginal right to hunt the Bathurst caribou herd, the GNWT did not prepare the necessary preliminary assessment and did not consult meaningfully and reasonably with the Métis.

R. v. Hirsekorn, 2013 ABCA 242

In 2007 Garry Hirsekorn killed a mule deer near the Cypress Hills in southeastern Alberta. When he was charged by the Province for hunting out of season and without a licence, he defended himself by asserting an Aboriginal right to hunt as a Métis person. The Alberta Court of Appeal concluded that Hirsekorn did not have to prove the existence of a historic Métis community in the vicinity of the location where he shot his deer or that the specific hunting location was integral to Métis culture. But, the court held, it wasn't sufficient for Hirsekorn to rely on the fact that historically the Métis had hunted in central and southern Alberta or generally throughout the plains. Instead, Hirsekorn had to prove that his ancestors frequented the Cypress Hills so that it was part of their "ancestral lands" or "traditional territory" for hunting before the arrival of the North-West Mounted Police in 1874. Because Hirsekorn had failed to prove this, he could not establish an Aboriginal right to hunt in the Cypress Hills.

Why It Matters

As the decision in *Enge* exemplifies, the threshold for triggering the Crown's duty to consult is relatively low. While the Métis have to point to evidence that fits the Aboriginal rights test laid down by the Supreme Court in *Powley* to trigger the Crown's duty, a credible claim will do, even if it might be unlikely to succeed in court. In contrast, the decision in *Hirsekorn* demonstrates how difficult it can be to establish an Aboriginal right in court, especially for the Métis of the Prairies. The *Powley* test was not designed to favour a highly mobile society with few documentary records.

One reason it is much more difficult to prove an Aboriginal right than it is to trigger the duty to consult is that the legal consequences are very different. Once triggered, the duty to consult doesn't necessarily lead to accommodation. If a claim is weak or the potential effects minimal, the legal obligation on the Crown may not be particularly onerous. But if an Aboriginal right is proven in court or otherwise recognized, or a First Nation has established treaty rights, governments may be required to do more than simply consult and perhaps accommodate. Depending on the circumstances, they may have to show that there is a valid reason to infringe the right, that they have infringed on the right as little as necessary and that they have given priority to the Indigenous people in exercising their right.

The differing requirements for triggering the duty to consult and for proving an Aboriginal right, and the different legal obligations on government that flow from each, underscore why Indigenous people with recognized Aboriginal and treaty rights should be cautious about agreeing to processes that require no more than consultation and, perhaps, accommodation. Recognized Aboriginal and treaty rights deserve respect—governments shouldn't diminish them by treating them the same as unrecognized or unproven Aboriginal rights.

Columbus's Ghost: Past Infringements and the Duty to Consult

When it comes to upholding the honour of the Crown, there is no clean slate. As much as governments may wish otherwise, Indigenous Peoples throughout Canada continue to demand recognition of and redress for past wrongs. The BC Court of Appeal's 2013 decision in *Louis v. British Columbia (Minister of Energy, Mines and Petroleum Resources)* exemplifies the continuing uncertainty over whether and when the duty to consult and accommodate is the proper forum for addressing unresolved infringements of Aboriginal rights, title and treaty rights.

In 1965 British Columbia authorized an open-pit molybdenum mine in Stellat'en territory about two hundred kilometres west of Prince George for an indefinite period. In 2003 the mine operator, Thompson Creek Metals, estimated the mine would close in approximately ten years. However, in 2007 Thompson Creek Metals decided to extend the life of the mine by expanding and modernizing its operations. Its plans required amendments to its primary mining permit as well as a series of other authorizations.

The Province restricted its consultation efforts with the Stellat'en to the specific new effects of each individual amendment and authorization required for the expansion.

The Stellat'en insisted on consultation on the proposed mine expansion as a whole and that it include the effects of the mine's forty-plus-year history of operations. The BC Supreme Court endorsed the Province's approach and the Stellat'en appealed.

The Court of Appeal concluded that because there was no high-level or strategic provincial decision requiring consultation on the project as a whole, the Province was correct to consult with the Stellat'en on a piecemeal basis, considering each permit or amendment application separately. Importantly, the Stellat'en did not identify any potential adverse effects due to the individual authorizations. Therefore, according to the court, the Province had fulfilled its legal obligation to consult.

While it acknowledged that the practical, cumulative effect of the Province's authorizations was to extend the life of the mine, the court held that this was not a new adverse impact on Stellat'en Aboriginal title and rights because the mining company had long ago acquired title from the Province to the land and the minerals.

Why It Matters

Across Canada, Indigenous Peoples endure the accumulated history of the denial of their Aboriginal rights, title and treaty rights. Whether the duty to consult applies to past, existing and ongoing infringements of these rights is one of the most important outstanding questions in Aboriginal law.

For over a hundred years, mines were dug, dams built and roads pushed through without serious consideration for the rights of Indigenous people. Following the Supreme Court's 2004 *Haida Nation* decision, Indigenous people began to consider whether the duty to consult and accommodate might open the door for addressing these past, existing and ongoing failures to consult and accommodate.

For some, the Supreme Court's 2010 *Rio Tinto* decision appeared to slam that door shut. The decision can and has been read to exclude past, existing and ongoing infringements from the duty to consult and accommodate. But, as the BC Court of Appeal observed in *West Moberly*, this is likely a misreading of the decision.

The Supreme Court in *Rio Tinto* was focused on the question of when the duty to consult arises, not the content of consultation once the duty is triggered. The court held that historic or past infringements on their own do not give rise to a fresh duty to consult. For those wrongs, Indigenous Peoples' only viable legal option is to sue the government for damages.

But the court in *Rio Tinto* left the door open on two important issues. First, the court clarified that it was not answering the question of whether continuing and ongoing infringements might trigger the duty to consult—that was an issue for another day. Second, the court indicated that if new adverse effects did trigger the duty to consult, a prior or continuing breach of the duty might be part of consultation and accommodation discussions.

Where does this leave the BC Court of Appeal's recent decision in *Louis*? The only way to read the decision as consistent with *Rio Tinto* and *West Moberly* is to understand it is another case, like *Rio Tinto*, primarily about whether there were new adverse effects on Stellat'en Aboriginal title and rights sufficient to trigger the duty to consult. The court concluded there were not. When the court in *Louis* commented that the Province did not have to include past infringements in the consultation process, it must have meant that this was because a fresh duty to consult had not been triggered. Otherwise, the decision is out of line with *Rio Tinto* and *West Moberly*.

The issue of so-called past infringements was finally clarified by the Supreme Court in its 2017 *Chippewas* decision, where it cited with approval the BC Court of Appeal's decision in *West Moberly* (see "The Duty to Consult at the Supreme Court in 2017" on page 110).

The wrongs of colonization are written on the lands of the Indigenous Peoples of Canada. Indigenous people witness and endure them on a daily basis. Whether the duty to consult and accommodate is capable of addressing these wrongs remains an open question.

The *Groundhog Day* Conundrum

If government had its way, the duty to consult would suffer the plight of Bill Murray in *Groundhog Day*—devoid of a past and a future, doomed to the confines of the present. In its June 2013 decision in *Adams Lake*, the BC Supreme Court made a further contribution to the developing law on whether there are past and future components to the duty to consult, with mixed results for government and First Nations.

In the 1960s Tod Mountain, an hour northeast of Kamloops, BC, was a local ski hill with one ski run and a rickety lift. In the early 1990s, encouraged by the provincial government's dreams of a series of Whistler-like ski resorts across the province, the Nippon Cable Company took control of the ski hill.

In 1993 the Province approved a Master Development Agreement (MDA) for a phased development over a 4,140-hectare area including numerous ski lifts and runs, a golf course, hiking and mountain biking trails and a village centre with condos, hotels, restaurants and shops. The Sun Peaks Resort was born.

At the time the MDA was approved, the provincial government's position was that Aboriginal title had long ago been extinguished through provincial legislation and that Aboriginal rights were of little consequence until proven in court. Given the Province's position, it is unsurprising that it gave no regard to the Secwepemc Nation's Aboriginal title and rights at the time it approved the MDA.

For nearly fifteen years, Secwepemc opposition to Sun Peaks, largely led by the Adams Lake Indian Band, was in and out of the news and the courts. The BC Supreme Court's 2013 decision was in regards to a challenge to the Province's decision to allow new ski runs and a ski lift to be built on Mount Morrisey.

What the Court Said

The duty to consult arises when the government contemplates conduct or a decision that will potentially affect Aboriginal title and rights. The first issue the court had to deal with was the Province's argument that there was no duty to consult because the approval of the new ski lift and runs was not really a decision. Instead, the Province was simply issuing approvals it had committed to in 1993 through its decision to approve the MDA. According to the Province, the Supreme Court of Canada in *Rio Tinto* held that there is no requirement to consult about past decisions (like the 1993 MDA decision), and, therefore, there was no need to consult about further approvals to expand Sun Peaks.

The court rejected this argument. The court held that the 1993 MDA had not authorized Sun Peaks to actually build anything—it still needed further operational approvals. The court reasoned that while subsequent operational decisions may have had a lesser effect on Aboriginal title and rights, and so warranted a lower level of consultation, this did not eliminate the requirement for consultation.

THE <font>GROUNDHOG DAY</font> CONUNDRUM

The court also reasoned that since the MDA required Sun Peaks to comply with all laws in force at the time a specific phase of the development proceeded, it now had to comply with the common law duty to consult, even if the duty had not yet been recognized in 1993. The Province could not shield itself from its obligation to consult based on its earlier, long-held assumption that it could issue authorizations to Sun Peaks regardless of First Nation interests.

The court also concluded that given there was no substantial consultation with Adams Lake when the MDA was approved in 1993, it would not be consistent with the honour of the Crown to allow the Province to now avoid consultation on operational decisions.

Although the court rejected the Province's argument that past injustices immunized it from a present-day obligation to consult, it also rejected Adams Lake's argument that consultation had to include possible future impacts of the continued development of Sun Peaks. The court reasoned that the authorizations for the ski lift and runs were an end in themselves. Any further future impacts would require additional authorizations. Consequently, it was reasonable and correct for the Province to restrict consultation to the effects of the current decisions.

Based on the specific facts of the level of consultation required and the adequacy of the Province's consultation and accommodation efforts, ultimately the court rejected Adams Lake's argument that the Province had failed to discharge its obligation to consult and accommodate before issuing the authorizations to develop Mount Morrisey.

Why It Matters

In the last several years, "past infringements" and cumulative effects have been at the forefront of the unresolved issues surrounding the duty to consult. Governments and companies have read the Supreme Court of Canada's decision in *Rio Tinto* as closing the door on the issue of past infringements. First Nations, supported by Chief Justice Lance Finch's reasons in *West Moberly*, have read *Rio Tinto* as leaving open the possibility of consultation including the effects of past decisions. Likewise, the law remains unsettled as to if and when the cumulative effects of a proposed project must be considered as part of the duty to consult.

The BC Supreme Court's 2013 decision in *Adams Lake* did not settle either of these questions. But it did make it more difficult for government to simply ignore the effect of past decisions while also increasing the challenge First Nations face when seeking consultation on the cumulative effects of a series of interrelated government decisions.

Breathing Life Back into the Duty to Consult

Since the Supreme Court of Canada's *Rio Tinto* decision in 2010, a growing number of court decisions have relied on a narrow interpretation of governments' obligations to consult and accommodate First Nations. In *Chartrand*, the British Columbia Court of Appeal pointedly rejected this approach by reminding everyone of some of the most important duty-to-consult decisions to come out of British Columbia over the last fifteen years.

In the early 1850s, Hudson's Bay Company fur traders, on behalf of Britain, negotiated treaties with Indigenous Peoples on Vancouver Island. Two of the treaties were with the predecessors of the Kwakiutl First Nation. They agreed to grant the HBC certain rights to a strip of land extending inland for three kilometres from the coast excluding their village sites and enclosed fields. They were also guaranteed the right to hunt on unoccupied lands and to carry on their fisheries as formerly. For over one hundred sixty years since, the Kwakiutl have struggled for recognition of their treaty rights and of their Aboriginal title and rights outside the three-kilometre-wide strip of land covered by their treaties.

In 2007 British Columbia removed private lands owned by Western Forest Products from the company's tree farm licence and approved a new forest stewardship plan in

Kwakiutl territory. In 2012 the forest stewardship plan was extended for an additional five years. While the Province consulted with the Kwakiutl about the effect of the decisions on the First Nation's treaty rights, it refused to consult in regards to the Kwakiutl's claims to Aboriginal title and rights outside the three-kilometre-wide treaty area.

The Kwakiutl filed a judicial review of the decisions on the basis that British Columbia had not properly consulted and accommodated them for the effect of the decisions on their Aboriginal title, rights and treaty rights. In 2013 the British Columbia Supreme Court decided against the Kwakiutl, concluding that the Province's efforts to consult in relation to the forestry decisions had been adequate and that, therefore, it had fulfilled its legal obligations. However, the court did grant the Kwakiutl a declaration that the Province was under an ongoing duty to consult with them in regards to their Aboriginal title and rights.

Both parties appealed to the BC Court of Appeal. The Province's position was that the lower court erred in granting the declaration of an ongoing duty to consult in regards to asserted Aboriginal title and rights. The Kwakiutl argued that the lower court erred in not concluding that the Province had breached the duty to consult and in not ordering the Province to involve the federal government in decisions affecting their Aboriginal title, rights and treaty rights.

What the Court Said

On the issue of the declaration granted by the lower court, the Court of Appeal agreed with the Province. The court concluded that the lower court had gone too far in granting the declaration. The court held that the declaration inappropriately and unnecessarily sought to describe the duty to consult and address issues that were not before the court. On the question of the adequacy of consultation, the court agreed with the Kwakiutl. The court held that the lower court had taken an overly narrow and technical approach to evaluating the adequacy of the Province's consultation.

Importantly, the court differentiated between judicial reviews of run-of-the-mill government decisions and judicial reviews of government decisions that trigger the duty to consult Aboriginal peoples. The latter must be informed by the honour of the Crown and the importance of promoting reconciliation. In those situations, the courts should not simply ask whether a decision was fair but, more fundamentally, whether the Crown's constitutional duty to consult and accommodate Aboriginal peoples had been fulfilled.

As an example of the lower court's problematic approach, the Court of Appeal concluded the judge had taken an overly narrow view of the type of impacts required to demonstrate an adverse effect on the Kwakiutl's interests. It was sufficient for the Kwakiutl to demonstrate that the Province's decisions affected their ability to participate in decision-making and their ongoing ability to influence government policy that affected their lands and resources.

Similarly, the Court of Appeal held that the lower court erred in concluding that the Kwakiutl were not entitled to "deep consultation" because there was a shortage of evidence of specific effects on their rights. The court held that high-level effects on decision-making can be sufficient to trigger government obligations for deep consultation.

Finally, the court held that the Kwakiutl could not be faulted for failing to participate in a consultation process premised on the erroneous assumption that their interests were limited to their treaty rights because fundamentally inadequate consultation processes do not preserve the honour of the Crown.

Why It Matters

The Court of Appeal's decision is important for several reasons. First, it dispenses with the dubious argument that it is impossible for treaty First Nations to also claim Aboriginal title and rights. The so-called "historical treaties" were negotiated at different times, in different places, for different reasons and with different outcomes. There is no legal or principled reason to assume that, given the circumstances, a First Nation's Aboriginal title and rights could not have survived the finalization of a treaty.

Second, the decision is another example of the courts rejecting a site-specific assessment of impacts on Aboriginal title, rights and treaty rights. The court confirmed that high-level, strategic decisions can not only trigger the duty to consult but can also necessitate deep consultation.

Third, the decision speaks to First Nation jurisdiction over their lands. The duty to consult includes First Nation participation in decision-making and policy development.

Fourth, the decision is a welcome reminder that when it comes to the duty to consult, not just any consultation process will do. Consultation processes must proceed from the correct basis and must include the possibility of accommodating legitimate Indigenous concerns. First Nations cannot be faulted for refusing to participate in a bankrupt consultation process.

Last and perhaps most importantly, the decision is a much-needed check to a growing tendency by some courts to take a narrow view of governments' obligations to consult and accommodate Indigenous Peoples. Relying on earlier decisions from British Columbia, the court reiterated that because the duty to consult is a constitutional obligation, governments must be held to a high standard.

The Duty to Consult—A Roadblock to Direct Action

In British Columbia, civil disobedience and the advancement of Indigenous Peoples' legal rights have gone hand in hand. There is a long history of Indigenous people, frustrated with government and business running roughshod over their Aboriginal rights and title, setting up roadblocks to stop resource development, especially logging. In a bitter twist of irony, First Nations' history of direct action has contributed to advancing the law so as to now deny Indigenous people the option of setting up roadblocks when all else fails.

Behn v. Moulton Contracting Ltd., 2013 SCC 26

The Behn family of the Fort Nelson First Nation in Treaty 8 have a trapline. The British Columbia provincial government issued forestry licences and a road permit to Moulton Contracting to log trees within the Behns' trapline. In the fall of 2006, the Behns set up a camp on the road to the proposed logging area, effectively stopping Moulton from logging.

Moulton filed a lawsuit against the Behns and the Fort Nelson First Nation seeking damages for interference with its logging operations. In defence to the lawsuit, the Behns wanted to argue that they were not properly consulted about the proposed logging and that it would infringe their Treaty 8 rights to hunt and trap.

Moulton successfully argued at the BC Supreme Court and the BC Court of Appeal that the duty to consult and treaty rights are collective rights of a First Nation and that individual members such as the Behns cannot rely on them as a defence when being sued for setting up a roadblock.

What the Court Said

The Supreme Court of Canada ruled against the Behns. The court held that the Crown's duty to consult is owed to a First Nation as a whole, not to individual members. Unless individual members are authorized to represent a First Nation, there is no obligation on government to consult with them.

However, the Supreme Court did leave open the possibility of individuals acting on their own to protect their treaty rights. The court noted that in certain situations, an individual First Nation member might have a special connection to exercising a treaty right in a particular part of a First Nation's territory. On this basis, individual members might be able to demand that government deal with them directly if there is a breach of treaty or infringement of treaty rights.

But in the case of the Behns, the Supreme Court held that even if they could have, as individuals, sought to enforce their treaty rights to hunt and trap, they should have done so by launching their own legal challenge to the forestry licences and road permit issued to Moulton, not through direct action. The court would not countenance the Behns setting up a roadblock and then defending themselves by relying on their treaty rights because, according to the court, that would endorse the type of "self-help remedy" that brings the administration of justice into disrepute.

Why It Matters

The decision will cause Indigenous people across the country to think twice before taking the law into their hands to protect their lands and culture by blocking access to resource companies and others who have government authorization to undertake development activities on their lands. But at the same time, the court's decision starts to open a door that up until now has appeared closed to Indigenous people.

The court's repeated description of Aboriginal and treaty rights as collective, not individual rights, has created a presumption that individual First Nation members cannot seek to enforce Aboriginal and treaty rights—this could only be done by a representative of the First Nation as a whole. The court's decision raises the possibility, in specific circumstances, of individual First Nation members opposing government activity based on an infringement or breach of their treaty rights. While it is unclear how many individual First Nation members have both the motivation and the means to act on their own to defend their treaty rights, they now have a legal argument for doing so.

But for the Behn family, and especially patriarch George Behn, the court's decision must have been a cruel irony. By this time in his late eighties, George continued to hunt and trap as his ancestors did before him. As the former chief of the Fort Nelson First Nation, George was part of a generation of First Nations leaders who protested while government and industry refused to respect Aboriginal and treaty rights. These leaders often stood alongside First Nations members who, out of desperation and commitment to principles, erected road-blocks to protest government inaction. This on-the-ground activism played an important role in developing Aboriginal law, including the Crown's obligations to consult and accommodate. Decades later, the presence of those new legal obligations, and the opportunity for Indigenous people to insist in court that they are enforced, undermined the Behn family's efforts to defend George's trapline from logging.

The Duty to Consult as an Ongoing Obligation

The BC Supreme Court's 2014 decision in *Taku River* is another example of the courts rejecting attempts by government and companies to narrow the applicability of the duty to consult and accommodate. In 2004 the Supreme Court of Canada in *Taku River* (the companion case to *Haida Nation*) held that the Province had adequately consulted the Taku River Tlingit First Nation (TRTFN) before issuing an environmental assessment certificate (EAC) for the Tulsequah Chief Mine in northwestern BC. Importantly, the Supreme Court assured TRTFN that as part of the Crown's ongoing duty to consult, they could expect to be consulted throughout the permitting, approval and licensing process for the proposed mine.

Skip ahead six years. By 2010, Redfern, the mine proponent, had gone into receivership and the property had been acquired by Chieftain Metals. The EAC had been renewed for a second and final five-year term and was set to expire in 2012 unless the Province decided the project had been "substantially started" as required under the provincial Environmental Assessment Act. If the project was deemed to have been substantially started, the EAC would be in effect for the life of the project unless cancelled or suspended.

In 2012 Chieftain applied for a determination that the project had been substantially started. Despite the fact that the

74

bulk of the work done on the site consisted of tree clearing and completing a gravel airstrip, the Province agreed with Chieftain. TRTFN filed for judicial review of the Province's decision.

The court concluded that *project* under the provincial Environmental Assessment Act means physical activities affecting the land environmentally. To be substantially started, a project needs to have been started in its essentials, i.e., in a real and tangible way. In deciding whether a project has been substantially started, the decision maker should focus on what has been done since the EAC was first issued and especially on whether there have been physical activities that have a long-term effect on the site.

The court then considered whether the Province had breached its constitutional duty to consult TRTFN. The Province had not consulted TRTFN—in fact, it had not even given TRTFN notice of the pending decision. TRTFN had only found out about the decision by accident months after it had been made.

The court rejected the Province's argument that the duty to consult had not been triggered because the decision would have no new physical effects. The court concluded that the decision would directly affect what would happen at the project site. A negative decision would mean that the project would not be built. A positive decision meant the EAC would be in effect for the life of the project, subject only to the Province's supervisory powers. Consequently, the court concluded that the duty to consult had been triggered and that the Province had breached the duty by not consulting TRTFN.

Finally, the court also concluded that because of the Province's long history of consulting with TRTFN before decisions were made that might affect their constitutional rights, the Province had violated the doctrine of legitimate expectations by failing to consult about the EAC.

The court ordered that the decision be made again and that TRTFN have forty-five days' notice to present whatever written submissions it wanted on the issue of whether the project had been substantially started.

Why It Matters

The decision is important for two main reasons. First, it is another example of the courts rejecting the Crown's attempts to evade its constitutional obligations by arguing that a decision was made long ago and there is nothing new to consider. As the Supreme Court of Canada stated in *Taku River*, the duty to consult is an ongoing obligation throughout the life of a project. When there is a new decision or conduct that might affect Aboriginal title and rights, the duty to consult is triggered.

Second, *Taku River* is an example of the lower courts responding to government and industry attempts to exploit even the slightest ambiguity in a Supreme Court decision. In its 2010 *Rio Tinto* decision, the Supreme Court, for the first time, considered the role of administrative tribunals, such as the National Energy Board, in the fulfillment of the Crown's duty to consult and accommodate. Due to an uncharacteristic lack of precision in its language, the court unintentionally sowed the seeds for an argument that in order to trigger the duty to consult a government decision must result in specific physical impacts on the ground. Despite the fact that it was extremely doubtful that the Supreme Court intended to establish this principle, especially since it is incompatible with *Haida Nation* (the court's foundational duty-to-consult decision), government and industry have repeatedly made the argument ever since. The BC Supreme Court's decision in *Taku River* is another example of the courts rejecting this interpretation of *Rio Tinto*.

The Age of Recognition: The Significance of the *Tsilhqot'in* Decision

The release of the *Tsilhqot'in* decision on June 26, 2014 marked the beginning of the post-denial period of Indigenous rights. Like any new day, promise and hope abounded. What the future will bring in response is up to all Canadians. And we can start by taking stock of what *Tsilhqot'in* means.

The dots-on-a-map theory of Aboriginal title is dead.

The Supreme Court confirmed that Aboriginal title can include territorial claims and that the occupation requirement for proof is not limited to intensive, regular use of small geographical sites (e.g., fishing spots and buffalo jumps). Rather, regular use of large swaths of land for traditional practices and activities (e.g., hunting, trapping and fishing) when coupled with exclusivity may be sufficient to ground a claim for Aboriginal title.

The implications are profound. Government's long-time myopic focus on dots on a map indicating specific sites of occupation is now indefensible. Indigenous Peoples are now able to seek recognition of their wider territorial claims. For those who are ultimately successful like the Tsilhqot'in, the change will be dramatic. Subject to "justifiable infringements," Indigenous Peoples have the legal rights to exclusively use and occupy their title lands, to benefit from their lands and to decide on how their lands will be managed. In other words, in large part they will enjoy the rights and privileges of their ancestors. Over a century of denial will be put to rest.

Tsilhqot'in is about more than how to prove Aboriginal title and what happens if you succeed. For Indigenous people across Canada, it is also about the here and now. Nowhere is this more obvious than in the context of the duty to consult, which obligates governments to consult about, and possibly accommodate, Aboriginal title before it is recognized or proven in court. The possibility of territorial claims for Aboriginal title based on traditional activities will shift the duty-to-consult equation in favour of Indigenous people. Government and industry will have to step up and acknowledge the new reality. The court in *Tsilhqot'in* confirmed that a failure to meaningfully consult and accommodate Indigenous Peoples could result in development projects being cancelled and government and industry being liable for damages.

As the court specifically stated, there is a simple and effective way for government and industry to avoid the uncertainty and risk they now clearly face—obtain the consent of Indigenous Peoples before you mess with their lands and resources.

The provinces have assumed a heavy burden.

By authorizing provincial laws to apply to Aboriginal title lands in *Tsilhqot'in*, the court made new law and saddled the provinces with hefty legal obligations. The court clarified that when Indigenous Peoples succeed in confirming their Aboriginal title, a province will not be able to simply apply provincial laws through box-ticking consultation; the province will be subject to the much more onerous burden of obtaining consent or justifying infringements.

The court's test for justifying infringements of section 35 rights has largely fallen by the wayside since its 2005 decision in *Mikisew* in favour of less onerous—and often unsatisfactory—consultation obligations. When the provinces awaken to the reality of what it really takes to meet the test of justifying an infringement, they may well regret the new responsibilities they have won based on *Tsilhqot'in*.

The implications extend beyond Aboriginal title. Based on the reasoning in *Tsilhqot'in*, in July 2014 the Supreme Court in *Grassy Narrows* opened the door to provinces regulating treaty rights if they can justify infringements through the same test. The days of shuffling treaty rights to the side through cookie-cutter duty-to-consult processes is hopefully at an end. Similar standards should also apply to uncontested Aboriginal rights.

Treaties—The Jig Is Up

Tsilhqot'in significantly affects treaty peoples in other ways, too. For Indigenous Peoples with pre-Confederation treaties (e.g., the Douglas Treaties on Vancouver Island and the Peace and Friendship Treaties in the Maritimes), the implications are obvious: their claims to Aboriginal title can now be pursued with renewed confidence, and their demands that government obtain their consent before exploiting their lands have new credibility.

Tsilhqot'in is also vitally important for Indigenous Peoples with one of the numbered treaties negotiated in Ontario, the

Prairies, British Columbia and the North since Confederation. Successive provincial and federal governments have proceeded for generations on the assumption that through these treaties, Indigenous Peoples ceded, released and surrendered their Aboriginal title to so-called Crown lands. Even as treaty people have widely and consistently maintained that their ancestors did nothing of the kind. For them, the numbered treaties have been about establishing respectful, mutually beneficial relationships. The court's endorsement in *Tsilhqot'in* of a liberal test for Aboriginal title encompassing territorial claims based on traditional Indigenous practices will embolden treaty peoples to refuse the language of "cede, release and surrender" while they assert Aboriginal title over their ancestral lands.

Tsilhqot'in also affirms that new government mandates for the British Columbia treaty process are necessary. It is hard to imagine why Indigenous people would join or continue to participate in the current process with its predetermined, non-negotiable government limitations when the reality and promise of Aboriginal title has been confirmed.

Now is the time to honour, thank and recommit.

We must honour those, both Indigenous and non-Indigenous, who did so much in the long struggle to have Aboriginal title recognized and confirmed but did not live to see their dreams realized. Thanks are also owed to the current generation who inherited the weight of their ancestors' efforts yet did not shrink from the responsibility. And a recommitment is owed to future generations to ensure that this remarkable success is not undermined by complacency. The Supreme Court has handed all Indigenous people a mighty victory—now is the time to see that the promise is realized.

Seven years later, *Tsilhqot'in* is still the only court case in Canada that has resulted in a declaration of Aboriginal title. Several new claims have been filed in different parts of Canada since 2014, including one by my Mi'kmaw clients for roughly one-third of New Brunswick. There have also been several claims filed by Indigenous Peoples for smaller parts of their territories as a way to counter resource extraction proposals that are being pushed through without their consent. In British Columbia, the most active, ongoing Aboriginal title claims are being pursued by Cowichan Tribes, the Haida Nation and Kwikwetlem First Nation.

One of the issues at play in many of these Aboriginal title claims, which was left unanswered in *Tsilhqot'in*, is the question of whether Indigenous Peoples can make an Aboriginal title claim for so-called private land. Another issue of particular interest is whether and how Aboriginal title applies to the foreshore and the seabed.

Provinces Burdened with Fulfilling Treaty Promises

After *Tsilhqot'in* was argued at the Supreme Court, but before the decision was released, the question of the provinces' power to infringe section 35 constitutional rights, that the "existing aboriginal and treaty rights of the aboriginal peoples of Canada are hereby recognized and affirmed," was again argued at the Supreme Court in the context of treaty rights as part of the *Grassy Narrows* appeal. The Supreme Court's *Grassy Narrows* decision of July 2014 places a heavy legal burden on provincial governments when they seek to exploit Indigenous lands covered by the historical treaties of Canada. The challenge now is for First Nations to hold the provinces to account.

Between 1871 and 1923, Canada negotiated eleven numbered treaties with First Nations across the country, including the Anishinaabe of Treaty 3 in Northwestern Ontario and Eastern Manitoba. With slight variations, many of the treaties allowed for the "taking up" of lands for non-Indigenous settlement, mining, logging and other purposes. The primary issue in *Grassy Narrows* is what limits exist on Ontario's ability to exercise the "taking up" clause in Treaty 3.

After the Ontario Court of Appeal overturned the trial decision in the case, Grassy Narrows First Nation and Wabauskang First Nation both appealed to the Supreme

Court. I acted as counsel for Wabauskang. We argued that the Court of Appeal erred by failing to confirm the federal government's role in implementing Treaty 3 based on both the specific wording of the treaty and Canada's exclusive responsibility for First Nations under the constitution.

The Supreme Court confirmed Ontario's unilateral authority to take up lands in the Keewatin area of Treaty 3 without federal government supervision. The court also confirmed Ontario has all the constitutional obligations of the Crown, is bound by and must respect the treaty, must fulfill treaty promises and must administer Crown lands subject to the terms of the treaty and First Nations' interest in the land.

Consequently, Ontario's exercise of its powers must conform with the honour of the Crown and is subject to the Crown's fiduciary duties when dealing with Aboriginal interests. When lands are intended to be taken up by Ontario, the Province must consult and, if appropriate, accommodate First Nations interests beforehand. Ontario must also deal with First Nations in good faith and with the intention of substantially addressing their concerns. It cannot exclude the possibility of accommodation from the outset.

As explained in the Supreme Court's 2005 *Mikisew* decision, if a "taking up" were to leave the First Nation with no meaningful right to hunt, trap or fish, a potential action for treaty infringement will arise. Finally, relying on its recent decision in *Tsilhqot'in*, the court held that if a "taking up" amounts to an infringement of the treaty, it is open to the Province to attempt to justify the infringement under the test laid down in *Sparrow* and *Badger*.

The basic requirements for justifying the infringement of Aboriginal title and for justifying the infringement of a treaty right are the same. First, the Crown must establish a compelling and substantial objective consistent with the Crown's fiduciary obligations to Indigenous Peoples. For a government objective to be compelling and substantial, it must be considered from both the public and the Indigenous perspective. It must also further the goal of reconciliation of Indigenous Peoples' rights and interests with the Crown's assertion of sovereignty over Indigenous lands.

In addition, the Crown must establish that the infringement of the treaty right is necessary to achieve the compelling and substantial objective. It must demonstrate that the infringement minimally impairs the treaty right and that the benefits to the general public are not outweighed by the negative impacts on the First Nation. As with Aboriginal title, the provinces should be expected to seek First Nations' consent for infringement of treaty rights. Without consent, authorizations may be quashed and damages awarded.

While technically a loss for Grassy Narrows and Wabauskang, the *Grassy Narrows* decision will most likely prove a powerful tool for ensuring that Ontario, and other provinces, respect treaty rights. The court was unequivocal that while Ontario can exercise its interests in Crown lands, its authority is subject to treaty and is burdened by the Crown's constitutional obligations, including fiduciary obligations.

The decision should be read as a companion case to *Tsilhqot'in*. There the court confirmed that unless they can obtain First Nation consent, the provinces must justify infringements of Aboriginal title—an extremely heavy legal burden.

Except for instances where lands are being "taken up," meaning put to a visibly incompatible use, based on *Grassy Narrows* it is now arguable that the provinces must also obtain First Nations' consent or justify infringements of treaty rights.

Ontario's win in *Grassy Narrows* has come at a high cost. Ontario and other provinces can now expect to be held to higher standards when seeking to develop Indigenous lands. Where before they were able to argue that their obligations were restricted to the less onerous duty to consult, they are now liable for the heavy burden of justifying infringements of treaty rights.

Environmental Assessments and the Duty to Consult

Lawyers are unrepentant armchair quarterbacks. We spend a lot of time politely and discretely wagging our fingers at the Supreme Court pointing out, from our perspective, its failure to grasp the subtlety of our arguments and dreaming of the day the court will update the law to coincide with our views. A likely measure of our intellectual shortcomings is how rarely this happens. For this reason, I have a special fondness for the Supreme Court's comments about environmental assessments and the duty to consult in its 2017 *Clyde River* decision because it gave me one of those rare moments when I could honestly say, "That's what I've been arguing for years!"

Dating at least as far back as the court's *Haida Nation* and *Taku* decisions in 2004, I've tilted at the environmental assessment windmill. My constant refrain to First Nations audiences has been "Don't simply accept an environmental assessment as a sufficient process for assessing impacts on your title and rights—you aren't Ducks Unlimited!"

With the approval of the courts (see the Supreme Court's 2004 *Taku* decision), federal and provincial governments often shoehorn the duty to consult and accommodate First Nations into environmental assessment processes. There are two fundamental problems with this approach. First, governments and proponents can easily manipulate the requirements for triggering an environmental assessment. By doing so, they all but eliminate the process for consulting with Indigenous people on a project's potential effects on their constitutionally protected rights.

This happened in 2013 when the federal government issued new draft regulations under the Canadian Environmental Assessment Act that significantly reduced the number of projects requiring a federal environmental assessment and, therefore, a government decision requiring consultation and accommodation. In 2020 the Ontario government similarly amended the Environmental Assessment Act to change the requirements for triggering an environmental assessment.

The BC Supreme Court's 2015 *Fort Nelson First Nation* sets out in detail how an environmental assessment triggering requirement can be manipulated to the detriment of Indigenous people. A proponent sought provincial government approval to develop the Komie North Mine near the City of Fort Nelson as a sand and gravel pit to supply fracking sand to the local oil and gas industry. There were indications that the proponent had plans to develop five more sand and gravel pits. All of these pits would be in the territory of the Fort Nelson First Nation, a member of Treaty 8.

Under the British Columbia Environmental Assessment Act, a new sand and gravel pit requires an environmental assessment if 500,000 tonnes or more of sand and gravel are excavated during one year or if over a four-year period a total of one million tonnes or more are excavated. The proponent was planning to excavate much more than one million tonnes of sand and gravel over four years from the Komie North Mine.

But, according to the proponent, it only intended to sell a small portion of the sand and gravel excavated. The rest would be waste. Therefore, the proponent informed the Province that the Komie North Mine would have a production capacity of not more than 960,000 tonnes of sand and gravel over a four-year period—40,000 tonnes less than the threshold to trigger a provincial environmental assessment.

Based on the proponent's estimate, and without consulting the Fort Nelson First Nation, the Province decided the Komie North Mine proposal did not meet the threshold to trigger an environmental assessment. The Fort Nelson First Nation applied for judicial review of the provincial government's decision on the basis that it was unreasonable and that the Province had failed to consult and accommodate.

Based on a BC Court of Appeal decision that had described provincial environmental assessments as "proponent driven," the Province argued that it was right to accept the proponent's production capacity estimate for Komie North Mine and was not required to look behind the numbers to determine if they were reasonable.

The court rejected the Province's uncritical acceptance of a proponent-driven approach to the issue of whether environmental assessments are triggered. According to the court, such an approach ran the risk of allowing projects that interfered with Aboriginal and treaty rights to proceed without environmental assessments. The possibility that a First Nation might subsequently succeed in having a proponent penalized would be of little or no benefit to a First Nation after its rights had been infringed or extinguished. According to the court, it was unreasonable for the Province to interpret its legislation to restrict the calculation of production for new sand and gravel pits to only that portion of the extracted sand and gravel the proponent intended to sell or use.

The court concluded that when constitutional rights are involved, the Province must be held to a higher standard to protect those rights than when it is considering general issues of environmental protection. The court noted that by accepting the proponent's limitation on the calculation of the mine's production capacity, the Province had set the stage for more mines to proceed without environmental assessments. Consequently, the decision potentially affected all areas in the Fort Nelson First Nation's territory with the potential for fracking sand mining.

Although the BC Supreme Court decision was subsequently set aside on appeal, it is a stark example of how by either setting higher triggering thresholds or favouring industry when deciding on whether a threshold has been met, governments can practically scope out the duty to consult. It is one of the clearest examples of the lower courts identifying how environmental assessments can be manipulated by governments and proponents to sidestep consultation with Indigenous people.

The problem with environmental assessments extends beyond the issue of whether they are triggered. Even when they do occur, they often fail to provide a meaningful forum for discharging the Crown's constitutional obligations to Indigenous people. This is because environmental effects are not the same as potential effects on Aboriginal rights. While in some cases there is a correlation between the two, they are not synonymous and should not be conflated. When asked about this, I cite two examples of Indigenous people's inherent and constitutionally protected rights that environmental assessments are not equipped to assess: the right to exercise Indigenous laws and decision-making authority and the right to benefit from the land. These rights are crucial to all First Nations. Because they do not equate with environmental effects, shoehorning the duty to consult into an environmental assessment process eliminates them from consideration from the outset.

With its 2017 *Clyde River* decision, the Supreme Court of Canada finally addressed the fundamental problem with environmental assessments (see "The Duty to Consult at the Supreme Court in 2017" on page 110). The court confirmed that assessing environmental impacts should not be conflated with the Crown's obligations to consult and accommodate effects on Indigenous Peoples' rights. The full range of potential impacts on Aboriginal rights must be assessed, regardless of their correlation with environmental impacts.

Any sense of vindication I felt from the court's *Clyde River* decision has been overtaken by deep frustration. Despite the Supreme Court of Canada's clear direction that the Crown's constitutional obligations to consult and accommodate Indigenous people cannot be simply subsumed within environmental assessment processes, this is exactly what continues to happen across Canada.

This fact underscores a deeper challenge faced by Indigenous people when they are forced to rely on the Canadian legal system. Even when they overcome the odds and the imbalance of power and resources between themselves and government and industry and wrest a favourable decision from the Supreme Court, the victory too often has little practical effect. Governments throw up numerous flimsy excuses for delays in "implementing" a Supreme Court decision or simply ignore it all together. For anyone doubting this is true, they need look no further than the federal government's shameful ongoing refusal to respect *Marshall*, the Supreme Court's twenty-one-year-old decision on Mi'kmaw commercial fishing rights. Canadians must demand better of their governments. If the rule of law is to mean anything in Canada, it has to start with Canadian governments following the laws of the country's highest court.

Is the Duty to Consult Clear as Mud?

Industry and its supporters complain that the duty to consult and accommodate is a murky mess with the courts failing to provide clarity. If only, they lament, the rules of engagement were clear and stable.

Their complaints are out of touch with reality.

Over fifteen years ago the Supreme Court set down the principles underpinning the duty to consult in simple and clear language in *Haida Nation*. At the same time, and for the benefit of First Nations, governments and industry, the court evaluated a specific consultation process in *Taku River* as an example of what was required to fulfill the duty to consult.

The court's subsequent decisions have simply clarified when the duty to consult applies. Sixteen years ago in *Mikisew* the court explained when the duty to consult applies to so-called historical treaties. In 2010 the court extended the duty to consult to modern treaties (*Beckman*) and clarified when and how the duty to consult applies to administrative tribunals and existing infringements (*Rio Tinto*).

For well over a decade, the Supreme Court's requirements for meaningful consultation and accommodation have been clear, known and consistent.

In *Haida Nation* the Supreme Court described its task as "establishing a general framework for the duty to consult and accommodate." It was up to lower courts to "fill in the details." The lower courts have done their work. With literally hundreds of duty-to-consult court decisions since *Haida Nation*, there is little room left on the canvas for anything new. The picture has been filled in, clarified and sharpened in detail over and over again. Anyone still unsure when and how the duty to consult is intended to apply has not done their homework.

Importantly, First Nations have borne the disproportionate burden of clarifying the law around the duty to consult and accommodate. Faced with governments that ignore the Supreme Court's clear directions, First Nations have been forced to expend their energy and limited resources on litigation to defend their Aboriginal title, rights and treaty rights. In court they are opposed by governments and companies with comparatively unlimited resources derived in large part from exploiting Indigenous lands.

The law of the duty to consult is clear and workable. Complaints from industry to the contrary smack of an underlying conflicting agenda. Similar to industry lobbyists' complaints of too much red tape, those who grumble that the law of the duty to consult has too much uncertainty likely mean there is just too much of the duty to consult. Instead of blowing smoke in our eyes with complaints about a lack of clarity surrounding the duty to consult, industry and its sympathizers should be pressing governments to live up to the spirit and intent of their constitutional obligations to Indigenous Peoples.

Implications of the *Tsilhqot'in* Decision

With Contributions from Kate Gunn

Prior to *Tsilhqot'in* and *Grassy Narrows*, it was understood that the Canadian federal government bore exclusive constitutional responsibility for regulating Aboriginal and treaty rights, and furthermore that the doctrine of interjurisdictional immunity operated to protect the federal government's exclusive role from provincial interference. As a result, until 2014 Indigenous Peoples could prevent provinces from infringing on Aboriginal and treaty rights.

In *Tsilhqot'in* and *Grassy Narrows*, the Supreme Court dramatically reduced the federal government's exclusive authority when a province proposes to undertake legislation or other activity that could affect Aboriginal and treaty rights. Now, provinces are allowed to attempt to justify infringements of Aboriginal title and rights.

The *Grassy Narrows* appeal centred on the issue of what limits exist on provinces that seek to take up land for forestry and other purposes pursuant to the numbered treaties. Based on its interpretation of Treaty 3 and the constitutional division of powers, the court held that the numbered treaties were with the Crown, not the federal government, and that provinces could "stand in Canada's shoes" with respect to the fulfillment and infringement of treaty rights.

Court decisions since *Tsilhqot'in* and *Grassy Narrows* suggest that courts are relying on these decisions to affirm the expansion of provincial jurisdiction over Aboriginal and treaty rights, and by extension, land and resource development. The decisions are contrary to many Indigenous Peoples' understanding that their relationship is with the Crown and that it is up to Canada, the federal government, to fulfill the Crown's obligations.

But the provinces might ultimately rue the day the court changed the law and increased provincial authority over Aboriginal and treaty rights. As the court explained in *Tsilhqot'in*, justifying an infringement of a section 35 right is no easy task. Except for instances where lands are already being taken up, it is now arguable that the provinces must obtain First Nations' consent or justify infringements of treaty rights that result from a provincial authorization.

Furthermore, many provincial decisions that affect treaty rights (e.g., the enforcement of wildlife and fishery laws, or the development of forest management plans) are not a taking up of land under treaty. In those instances, provincial governments would need to meet the requirements for justifying the infringement of the treaty rights.

The provinces now have clear responsibility for fulfilling outstanding treaty promises and can no longer hide behind the federal government's inaction. For example, the provinces have long taken the position that when treaty lands are owed Indigenous people, they will transfer the land, but loss-of-use compensation owed to Indigenous people is the responsibility of the federal government. *Tsilhqot'in* and *Grassy Narrows* underscore the hollowness of the provinces' position. Having benefited from the failure to provide treaty lands, the provinces should acknowledge their responsibility to compensate Indigenous people.

Tsilhqot'in and *Grassy Narrows* also call into question governments' assumption that the historical treaties were "cede, release and surrender" treaties under which First Nations agreed to give up title to their lands. Given that both Indigenous Peoples and the Crown are constrained by the necessity of preserving Aboriginal title lands for the use and benefit of future generations, can the *common* intention of the treaties have been to extinguish Aboriginal title? Also, interpreting the treaties as extinguishment documents would be inconsistent with the Supreme Court's discussion in *Tsilhqot'in* and *Grassy Narrows* of the Crown's fiduciary obligations and the honour of the Crown.

As with most Supreme Court Aboriginal law decisions, it remains to be seen how lower courts will interpret and apply *Tsilhqot'in* and *Grassy Narrows*, especially in relation to treaty rights. While together the decisions provide the basis for renewed respect for the spirit and intent of historical treaties, the Supreme Court may eventually be called on to clarify the extent of the provinces' obligations and the limits on their authority.

Canada's Misguided Land Claims Policy

Following the *Tsilhqot'in* decision, in the fall of 2014 the federal government, through its ministerial special representative Douglas Eyford, sought comments on its new Interim Comprehensive Land Claims Policy. The interim policy set out Canada's position on negotiating with Indigenous Peoples over their Aboriginal title and rights. Unfortunately, the new policy was based on the same misguided objectives that have plagued Canada's approach to reconciliation for decades.

Colonization as Reconciliation

According to the federal government, the objective of its new land claims policy was to reconcile Indigenous Peoples' Aboriginal title and rights with the interests of non-Indigenous Canada. From the federal government's perspective, reconciliation is about achieving "certainty" for "economic and resource development." The focus on reconciliation as a process for non-Indigenous people to exploit Indigenous Peoples' lands and resources is an example of what John Ralston Saul described in *The Comeback* as the national narrative of colonization. Rather than acknowledge Indigenous lands as being integral to the survival of Indigenous Peoples as prosperous, self-sufficient societies, successive federal governments have viewed Indigenous lands from the perspective of the country's southern, non-Indigenous society—as "a source of commodities, colonial territories that will make those of us in the south rich."

Extinguishment Is Not the Answer

Canada's new land claims policy of 2014, like all the policies that preceded it, focused on the negotiation of treaties that extinguish Indigenous Peoples' interests in their lands in exchange for a lesser interest over a fraction of their territory. Reconciliation does not require extinguishment. The Supreme Court in *Tsilhqot'in* acknowledged that the reconciliation of Indigenous and non-Indigenous interests may be achieved through negotiating agreements that recognize, rather than extinguish, Aboriginal title.

Canada's Flawed Approach

Rather than negotiate agreements that recognize Aboriginal title, Canada decided to continue with a policy that is incompatible with the fundamental principles of Aboriginal title. As the court explained in *Tsilhqot'in,* Aboriginal title is a collective title held for the benefit of present and future generations of Indigenous people. The obligation to preserve Aboriginal title lands for future generations gives rise to an inherent limit: nothing can be done to Aboriginal title lands that would disentitle future generations' use and enjoyment of the land. Both the use of Aboriginal title lands by the current generation of Indigenous people and the possible infringement of Aboriginal title by the Crown are subject to this inherent limit. Canada's objective of achieving "certainty" through extinguishment is anathema to the very basis for Aboriginal title.

A policy of extinguishment is also inconsistent with the federal government's fiduciary responsibilities to Indigenous Peoples. The court in *Tsilhqot'in* affirmed that when dealing with Aboriginal title, Canada must respect its fiduciary responsibilities to Indigenous Peoples. At its core, this means ensuring that the federal government's actions are consistent with the best interests of Indigenous Peoples. A land claims policy intended to deprive future generations of Indigenous people of the use and benefit of their traditional lands by extinguishing Aboriginal title is incompatible with Canada's fiduciary obligations.

Reconciliation Based on Recognition

The way out of the narrative of marginalization of Indigenous Peoples and the exploitation of their lands is for Canada to adopt a land claims policy consistent with the principles underlying the United Nations Declaration on the Rights of Indigenous Peoples (UNDRIP) and the Supreme Court's *Tsilhqot'in* decision. At their heart UNDRIP and *Tsilhqot'in* are vehicles for Indigenous Peoples to prosper as distinctive societies by regaining control of their lands. They are predicated on the recognition of Indigenous Peoples' historical and legal interests in their lands, their right to decide how their lands are developed (or not developed) and their right to benefit from their lands.

For decades the federal government has justified its land claims policy of extinguishment by arguing that we really do not know what Aboriginal title means or that it even exists. *Tsilhqot'in* and UNDRIP have nullified these self-serving excuses for depriving present and future generations of Indigenous people of their lands. It is long past time that Canada jettisoned its colonization objectives and adopted a land claims policy intended to achieve reconciliation through agreements that lead to Indigenous Peoples controlling and benefiting from their lands.

In 2018 the federal government expressed an intention to move away from its existing comprehensive land claims policy, including its long-standing insistence on extinguishment, and to begin instead to finally start to recognize and implement Indigenous rights. This included establishing new "Principles Respecting the Government of Canada's Relationship with Indigenous Peoples" and a "Directive on Civil Litigation Involving Indigenous Peoples" to guide the recognition and implementation of Indigenous rights going forward. This new framework has resulted in the creation of dozens of "Recognition of Indigenous Rights and Self-Determination" discussion tables across the country. The jury is still out on whether the federal government has actually changed its policies or whether Indigenous people are once again being offered rhetoric over substance.

The Duty to Consult—A Narrow Vision

First Nations across Canada are frustrated with a lack of land use planning and consideration for the cumulative environmental effects of development on their lands. The 2015 *Yellowknives Dene First Nation v. Canada* decision from the Federal Court of Appeal exemplifies their concerns and illustrates how difficult it is to get the courts to address them.

The Drybones Bay area on the north shore of Great Slave Lake in the Northwest Territories is of great importance to the Yellowknives Dene First Nation. In recent years it has also become the focus of increasing mineral exploration. Local First Nations have repeatedly warned that their Aboriginal and treaty rights are being eroded due to the cumulative environmental effects of various projects and a lack of land use planning.

While considering an application for an earlier project, the Mackenzie Valley Environmental Impact Review Board recommended to the federal government that a plan of action be developed for the area and that it include a cumulative effects assessment and substantial input from First Nations. The federal government rejected the review board's recommendation.

Subsequently, the review board considered a mining company's application for a five-year diamond exploration program in the Drybones Bay area. The review board decided the project would not have significant environmental effects and did not require an environmental impact review.

The Yellowknives Dene First Nation's application for judicial review of the review board's decision was dismissed by the Federal Court. The First Nation appealed to the Federal Court of Appeal.

The Court of Appeal rejected the First Nation's argument that the review board had failed to consider the cumulative effects of the diamond exploration program. According to the Court of Appeal, the review board had considered potential environmental effects, including cumulative effects, and had concluded it would not have significant adverse impacts because it was largely over water and because the lands had already been disturbed by earlier developments. The court held that the review board's findings were not unreasonable because they were supported by the evidence and were within the range of possible outcomes.

The Court of Appeal also rejected the First Nation's argument that the duty to consult and accommodate had not been fulfilled because the review board lacked the authority to mandate land use planning in the Drybones Bay area. The court held that the review board's conclusion that the project was unlikely to adversely affect the environment meant that land use planning was not necessary to accommodate the First Nation's concerns.

Why It Matters

By refusing to seriously consider cumulative effects as part of the duty to consult, and by limiting consultation to discrete decisions without acknowledging overall project impacts, governments across the country are sanctioning the piecemeal infringement and extinguishment of Indigenous Peoples' constitutional rights.

Land use planning that respects Indigenous jurisdiction, knowledge and values would address this serious issue. But, as the *Yellowknives* decision illustrates, without control over their lands, First Nations are dependent on government's willingness to support First Nation–driven land use planning. Unfortunately, governments either impose their own narrow, self-serving vision of land use planning (Ontario's Far North Act is an example), or they reject land use planning altogether.

The *Yellowknives* decision also illustrates the challenges for First Nations in achieving effective results through the courts. When governments follow the minimum procedural requirements for consultation, even if they do not take meaningful steps to address First Nation concerns that arise from the consultation, it is difficult for First Nations to persuade the courts to intervene.

On questions of fact, the courts defer to government decision makers. They ask whether consultation was adequate, whether there is any evidence to support a government decision and whether the decision was in the range of possible outcomes. These are relatively low hurdles for governments to overcome.

As the Supreme Court has stated, the duty to consult and accommodate is a constitutional imperative. It includes an obligation on both provincial and federal governments to engage with First Nations in good faith with the intention of meaningfully addressing their concerns. Until lower courts consistently apply these principles, many First Nations will continue to be left frustrated and disappointed with the duty to consult.

Good News for the Duty to Consult

The duty to consult and accommodate isn't a blunt instrument. For it to work, First Nations and government must be willing to participate in an open process of information sharing and honest listening. They must make good faith attempts to negotiate effective and responsive agreements.

Too often, governments fail to live up to their end of the bargain. Instead of meaningful engagement, they smother First Nations with hollow procedural niceties. Rather than work on solutions, they work on developing their consultation logs.

Most First Nations caught in a duty-to-consult house of mirrors have little recourse. They lack the resources to take governments to court. Those that manage to muster a legal challenge often face another obstacle—judges with a restricted view of government's obligations to consult and accommodate First Nations.

Several court decisions have offered a welcomed correction to governments' and judges' often narrow vision of the duty to consult. This can be seen most clearly in decisions focused on the question of what specific government action or decision-making triggers the duty.

Skip Ahead If Case Law Bores You

In *Huron-Wendat Nation*, the Federal Court was faced with a challenge to an agreement-in-principle (AIP) between Canada and Innu First Nations. Applying a generous and purposive approach to the question of whether the duty to consult had been triggered by the AIP, the court concluded on December 1, 2014 that it was obvious the AIP had an inevitable impact on the Huron-Wendat and therefore Canada should have consulted them before it was signed.

Also in December 2014, in *Courtoreille*, the Mikisew Cree First Nation's challenge to the Harper government's first and second omnibus bills, the Federal Court held that while Mikisew Cree had not demonstrated any actual on-the-ground harm to Aboriginal rights due to the legislation, a reasonable person would recognize the potential risk. This was sufficient to trigger the duty to consult and accommodate.

While on January 9, 2015, the Federal Court of Appeal in *Hupacasath* dismissed a challenge to Canada's foreign investment promotion and protection agreement (FIPA) with China, it endorsed a generous approach to the question of when the duty to consult arises that emphasizes the purpose of the duty to consult. The court emphasized that the duty is intended to prevent a present, real possibility of harm caused by government's dishonourable conduct. If a government agreement, such as a FIPA, raised the prospect of a future decision and it was possible to estimate the probability of that decision adversely affecting Aboriginal rights, the agreement would trigger the duty to consult.

STANDOFF

The most pointed recent rejection of a narrow view of the duty consult is found in the British Columbia Court of Appeal's 2015 *Chartrand* decision. Faced with the lower court's approval of the provincial government's refusal to consult with the Kwakiutl First Nation about its unrecognized Aboriginal title and rights on Vancouver Island, the Court of Appeal went back to first principles. It faulted the lower court for taking a restricted view of the duty to consult and reminded the Province that to uphold the honour of the Crown its processes must demonstrably promote reconciliation.

The Quebec Court of Appeal's 2014 criticism in *Corporation Makivik* of the provincial government's failure to adhere to the spirit and intent of the James Bay Agreement similarly emphasized that the duty to consult cannot be reduced to mindless procedures. For it to be meaningful, government must engage with First Nations with a "sufficiently open mindset."

The Federal Court of Appeal struck a similar note in *Long Plain* (2015), its review of the federal government's process for selling the Kapyong Barracks in Winnipeg. The court criticized Canada for taking an overly narrow, technical review of its obligations. Government consultation, said the court, must be imbued by honour, reconciliation and fair dealing.

Back to the Interesting Stuff

Too often governments and the courts lose sight of the special place of the duty to consult in Canadian law. Recent court decisions reminding us of the broader principles and purpose of the duty to consult and accommodate are an important recourse. As the BC Court of Appeal noted in *Chartrand*, when a government decision is challenged on the basis of the duty to consult, the courts should not simply ask whether the decision was fair. More importantly, the courts must ask whether government by its conduct has actively sought to promote reconciliation. This demanding standard is necessary because the duty to consult is not simply an administrative requirement—it is a constitutional imperative. The more often government decision makers recognize this higher obligation, and courts enforce it, the closer we will come to recognizing and respecting Indigenous Peoples' central legal, historical and future place in Canadian society.

Court Decisions Referred To

Canada v. Long Plain First Nation, 2015 FCA 177
Chartrand v. British Columbia, 2015 BCCA 345
Corporation Makivik c. Québec (Procureure générale), 2014
    QCCA 1455
Courtoreille v. Canada, 2014 FC 1244
Hupacasath First Nation v. Canada, 2015 FCA 4
Huron-Wendat Nation of Wendake v. Canada, 2014 FC 1154

The Duty to Consult at the Supreme Court in 2017

In 2017 the Supreme Court released four decisions that elaborated on the substance and application of the duty to consult and accommodate: *Clyde River (Hamlet) v. Petroleum Geo-Services*, 2017 SCC 40; *Chippewas of the Thames First Nation v. Enbridge Pipelines*, 2017 SCC 41; *First Nation of Nacho Nyak Dun v. Yukon*, 2017 SCC 58; and *Ktunaxa Nation v. British Columbia*, 2017 SCC 54. Based on these four decisions, below I summarize the court's thinking on the duty to consult on specific issues and offer my own thoughts on what it means for the present and future regarding the duty to consult.

Delegation

Governments, provincial and federal, delegate many decisions to tribunals which, like courts, consider evidence and hear submissions from applicants and intervenors before rendering their decisions. Soon after the Supreme Court's 2004 *Haida Nation* decision, the question arose as to what, if any, responsibility these administrative tribunals had to ensure that the duty to consult is fulfilled.

The first major legal pronouncements on the issue were from the BC Court of Appeal in 2009 with *Kwikwetlem First Nation v. British Columbia (Utilities Commission)* and *Carrier*

Sekani Tribal Council v. British Columbia (Utilities Commission). The latter decision was appealed to the Supreme Court and became *Rio Tinto v. Carrier Sekani Tribal Council,* 2010.

Delegation Principles

In *Chippewas* and *Clyde River,* the court, relying on *Rio Tinto,* confirmed established principles, added further detail and answered outstanding questions regarding administrative tribunals and the duty to consult. The court explained:

- an administrative tribunal's decision alone may be sufficient to trigger the duty to consult (i.e., a government department's involvement is not necessary);
- the Crown can rely wholly or in part on an administrative tribunal to fulfill the duty to consult;
- an administrative tribunal can be involved in consultation and accommodation and also decide whether the duty has been fulfilled;
- it must be made clear to First Nations that the Crown intends to rely on the administrative tribunal's processes as part of fulfilling the duty to consult;
- if the Crown intends to rely on an administrative tribunal to completely discharge the duty to consult, the tribunal must have the necessary statutory powers to fulfill the duty;
- the Crown always holds ultimate responsibility for ensuring that consultation and accommodation is adequate;
- when First Nations who are parties to modern treaties consider that an administrative tribunal's process is

inadequate to fulfill the Crown's duty to consult, they
should communicate directly with government and
request direct Crown engagement in a timely manner;
- once the duty to consult is triggered, an administrative tribunal can only proceed to make a decision if
consultation is adequate;
- the central question is whether the administrative tribunal has the required powers in the specific case to
fulfill the duty to consult;
- if an administrative tribunal lacks the requisite powers to fulfill the duty to consult, it should suspend
its processes or deny a requested authorization until
government has stepped in to meet the outstanding
obligations; and
- if the administrative tribunal does not have the necessary powers to fulfill the duty to consult or does not
provide adequate consultation and accommodation,
the Crown must provide further avenues for consultation prior to any approvals—otherwise the decision
can be quashed by the courts.

Implications

First, while the court referred specifically to First Nations
with modern treaties and their right to seek direct consultation with the Crown, there is no reason why the same principle would not apply to all First Nations, including those
without treaty or with so-called historical treaties.

Also, there is no reason why this principle should not
apply in all situations when the Crown delegates the duty to

consult, including when the government delegates the procedural aspects of the duty to third party proponents. In the past, lower courts have failed to accept that First Nations have a right to direct consultation with the Crown (see, for example, *Wabauskang First Nation v. Minister of Northern Development and Mines*, 2014). The court's comments on this issue are important for First Nations across the country who are frustrated with the delegation of the duty to consult and government's unwillingness to become directly involved.

Second, the court's confirmation that an administrative tribunal cannot proceed to make a decision if it lacks the powers to ensure adequate accommodation confirms a principle from *Rio Tinto* that potentially has wide-ranging application. There is no reason why this principle should not apply in all situations when a government decision maker contemplates making a decision that triggers the duty to consult. For example, the principle should extend to municipalities, which routinely make decisions that trigger the duty to consult. Consequently, the Supreme Court's reasoning in *Chippewas* and *Clyde River* likely undercut the precedential value of *Neskonlith Indian Band v. Salmon Arm (City)*, 2012, the leading lower-court decision on the issue of the duty to consult and municipalities.

Finally, the question of whether an administrative tribunal can be involved in fulfilling the duty to consult and ultimately decide whether the duty has been fulfilled has been lurking on the margins of duty-to-consult law for many years. In essence, the court in *Chippewas* held that an administrative tribunal can wear both hats because tribunals often carry out overlapping functions while remaining a neutral arbiter. The court's reasoning is circular and unconvincing. We should not assume that this is the final word on a thorny and important issue.

Accommodation

Accommodation is the Achilles' heel of the duty to consult. First Nations' frustration with the duty to consult is due to their first-hand experience with endless talk and little action. As long as meaningful accommodation remains elusive and only approached through sustained and dogged effort on the part of First Nations, the duty to consult will continue to sow frustration and cynicism.

Accommodation and Administrative Tribunals

In *Chippewas*, the court concluded that on the specific facts before it, the National Energy Board (NEB) had the necessary statutory powers to impose required conditions on the pipeline company as part of accommodation and therefore was able to fulfill the duty to consult. The implications of the court's narrow and specific conclusion on this point are important for companies, the NEB, other administrative tribunals and First Nations.

Contrary to the assumptions of many commentators, *Chippewas* is not a wholesale endorsement of the NEB's processes and ability to discharge the Crown's duty to consult. Depending on the facts of other projects and the required depth of consultation for those projects, the NEB might not have the necessary statutory powers required to accommodate

First Nations. When such a case arises, the law is clear: the NEB will not be able to make a decision until the federal government steps in and fulfills the Crown's outstanding constitutional obligations.

This principle applies to all administrative tribunals (and logically to all government decision makers). Before making a decision they must correctly gauge the required depth of consultation for a specific project, decide on the necessary accommodation measures (if any) and ensure that either they have the statutory powers to realize the required accommodation or that government does so through a parallel process. Until these steps are taken, they cannot decide.

Accommodation and Balancing of Interests

One of the central problems with the duty to consult and accommodate is that all too often the focus is on consultation, not accommodation. With varying success, First Nations fight hard to secure meaningful accommodation through negotiations. One of the challenges they increasingly face is the argument that their rights must be "balanced" with the wider public interest.

In 2017 the court reiterated two important points on this issue. First, neither broader economic interests nor the public interest trumps the Crown's obligations to consult and accommodate First Nations. If the duty to consult is not fulfilled, a project cannot be in the public interest. Second, because unproven and unrecognized Aboriginal rights do not give First Nations a veto as part of the duty to consult, the Crown and its agents are under a special responsibility to accommodate First Nations.

In regard to the veto question, in 2017 the court reiterated an important point it made over twenty years ago in *Delgamuukw* that governments and companies too often overlook. When consultation is based on a First Nation's unproven, unrecognized claims, the First Nation does not have a veto. But in certain cases, First Nation consent might be required when the duty to consult is triggered by proven claims.

Reasonableness and Accommodation

For First Nations who succeed in forcing meaningful accommodation negotiations, the question quickly arises: How strong is their negotiation position? In *Ktunaxa*, the court went further than in any previous decision in emphasizing the importance of First Nations not taking "unreasonable" positions.

The court criticized the Ktunaxa for taking what it described as an uncompromising and absolute position that left no room for negotiation and accommodation, and warned First Nations against taking "unreasonable positions."

There are two problems with the court's reasoning. First, why should one party in negotiations get to undermine and dismiss the position of the other party by simply labelling it "unreasonable"?

Second and most importantly, applying a reasonableness test to a First Nation's demands for accommodation would drastically narrow the scope of the duty to consult. It would exclude the most serious infringements and intractable disputes from the duty to consult, and limit the duty to addressing impacts on First Nation rights that can be readily accommodated. This cannot have been the court's intention in *Ktunaxa*.

A final word on reasonableness. The more the court narrows the duty to consult by relying on concepts of "adequacy" and "reasonableness," the further the court drifts away from its earlier descriptions of the duty as a constitutional imperative that must be met. By the time duty to consult is twisted and contorted based on "reasonableness" and "adequacy," the duty becomes a pale shadow of the court's lofty rhetoric. If the court continues to undermine the scope and effectiveness of the duty to consult for unproven and unrecognized rights, First Nations will increasingly choose to litigate to establish their rights instead of wasting their time consulting over unrecognized rights.

Existing Infringements

The question of whether the duty to consult and accommodate applies to existing infringements and cumulative effects has been at the centre of many lower court decisions over the last ten years. Governments and companies usually take the view that the duty is limited to new impacts arising from a new decision, while First Nations argue that it is illogical and dishonourable to ignore the wider context.

In *Chippewas* the Supreme Court reiterated and clarified a simple point it first made in *Rio Tinto* but has since been often lost or misunderstood. While existing infringements on their own do not trigger the duty to consult, once the duty is triggered by new potential impacts, the scope of the ensuing consultation and accommodation may be informed by cumulative effects and the historical context. On this issue, the court cited with approval Chief Justice Finch's reasons in *West Moberly First Nations v. British Columbia (Chief Inspector of Mines)*, 2011. By reiterating its reasoning from *Rio Tinto* and endorsing the approach taken in *West Moberly*, hopefully the court has put an end to the simplistic argument that the duty to consult is blind to existing infringements and cumulative effects.

Environmental Assessments

A source of continuing frustration for First Nations has been governments' persistent conflation of duty-to-consult processes with environmental assessments. While governments are free to rely on existing procedures and processes, including environmental assessments, as part of their efforts to fulfill the duty to consult, this should not change the focus and purpose of the engagement. In *Clyde River* the court criticized the National Energy Board for mistakenly focusing its inquiry on whether the project would cause significant environmental effects. The court confirmed what First Nations have been saying for years: when the duty to consult is triggered, a consideration of environmental effects alone will not do—the Crown must assess potential impacts on Aboriginal and treaty rights. A standard environmental assessment alone is unlikely to fulfill the duty to consult.

Remedy

Charles Dickens' Oliver Twist famously pleaded for more gruel. All too often First Nations have found themselves in similar circumstances with the duty to consult. Having expended their limited resources and succeeded against the odds in convincing a judge that government failed to live up to its constitutional obligations, their "win" often means another serving of the thin gruel of the duty to consult that left them dissatisfied in the first place.

From a legal perspective, the problem is one of remedy— what action should the courts take when governments fail to fulfill the duty to consult? Beginning with its 2014 decisions in *Grassy Narrows* and *Tsilhqot'in*, the Supreme Court has moved decisively to clarify the law on remedy. A decision that affects Aboriginal and treaty rights and does not comply with the duty to consult should be quashed. Moreover, litigation is not an opportunity for further consultation and, when a government is found to have failed to consult and accommodate, it does not simply get a do over—there are no mulligans.

The importance of the court's clear direction on this issue should not be lost on governments and proponents. It is no longer acceptable for governments and companies to take a minimalist approach to the duty to consult on the assumptions that a First Nation is unlikely to challenge them in court and that even if a court does find against them, they will get a second chance to make it right. They now face the real possibility of projects being cancelled and all the loss and uncertainty that would result.

Summing Up

There were major advancements in duty-to-consult law in 2017. The Supreme Court's confirmation that the permissible degree of delegation of the duty is limited by the decision maker's ability to accommodate is important for all decision makers to be aware of, not just administrative tribunals. Equally important is the court's endorsement of parallel, direct engagement processes with the Crown, something that First Nations have been demanding for years.

Meaningful accommodation continues to be the thorn in the side of the duty to consult. While the court in 2017 took an important step forward by confirming that governments don't simply get a do over and that authorizations should be quashed when they fail to properly consult and accommodate, its emphasis on the "reasonableness" of First Nations' demands may ultimately be seen as two steps back.

Change of Direction Required:
Mikisew Cree First Nation v. Canada

With Kate Gunn

In October 2018 the Supreme Court of Canada released its long-awaited decision in *Mikisew Cree First Nation v. Canada (Governor General in Council)*, 2018 SCC 40.

The court held that the Crown's duty to consult Indigenous Peoples prior to decisions that could affect their Aboriginal rights and treaty rights does not extend to the development of legislation. Accordingly, while it may be good policy for the government to consult prior to enacting legislation, there is no constitutional obligation to consult, and possibly accommodate, Indigenous Peoples about laws which could affect their section 35 rights.

Mikisew underscores the limited utility of the duty to consult and accommodate and the necessity for Indigenous Peoples to explore other ways to ensure that their rights and jurisdiction are respected.

What It's About

In 2012, the federal government introduced two pieces of omnibus legislation into the House of Commons that included significant changes to federal environmental protection legislation. The Crown did not consult Mikisew Cree First Nation about how the amendments could affect their rights under Treaty 8 at any stage of the development of the legislation.

Mikisew brought an application for judicial review on the basis that the Crown failed to discharge its constitutional duty to consult prior to enacting legislation which would impact Mikisew's treaty rights to hunt, fish and trap.

The Federal Court agreed with Mikisew and granted a declaration that the duty to consult was triggered in respect of the omnibus bill. On appeal, the Federal Court of Appeal found that the lower court erred in conducting a judicial review of the legislative action because in developing policy, ministers are acting in a legislative capacity and are therefore immune from judicial review. Mikisew appealed to the Supreme Court.

What the Court Said

The Supreme Court unanimously held that the ministerial development of legislation cannot be subject to judicial review by the courts. On the larger question of the application of the duty to consult, the majority of the court found that the duty is not triggered by the development of legislation, even where it has the potential to affect Indigenous Peoples' Aboriginal rights and treaty rights. Two members of the court held that the Crown's duty extends to all government decisions, including the development of law.

The Majority

The majority of the court held that the duty to consult is not triggered by the development of legislation, including because recognizing a duty to consult in the law-making process would require courts to improperly trespass on the legislative arm of government and lead to inappropriate judicial incursion on the workings of the legislature.

The court also held that recognizing a constitutionally mandated duty to consult in the process of legislation would be highly disruptive to the legislative process and could "effectively grind the day-to-day internal operations of government to a halt." Consequently, the court concluded that prior to the enactment of legislation, there is no constitutional obligation to consult Indigenous Peoples about how that legislation could affect their Aboriginal rights and treaty rights.

Importantly, the court emphasized that just because the duty to consult was not triggered in relation to the development of legislation, this did not absolve the Crown of its obligation to conduct itself honourably. The fact that the legislative process is not subject to judicial review should not "diminish the value and wisdom" of consulting Indigenous Peoples prior to enacting legislation that has the potential to adversely impact their Aboriginal rights and treaty rights, even where there is no recognized constitutional obligation to do so.

The Dissent

Justices Abella and Martin dissented on the issue of whether the duty to consult was triggered in the context of the legislative process. They held that the honour of the Crown gives rise to a duty to consult that applies to all contemplated government conduct with the potential to affect Aboriginal rights and treaty rights, including legislative action. To hold otherwise would create a void in the honour of the Crown and leave Indigenous Peoples vulnerable to the government carrying out processes that could affect their section 35 rights through legislative rather than executive action.

They also rejected the majority's view that extending the duty to consult to legislative action would be unworkable or cause undue interference by the courts in the legislative process. They noted that in many cases, a declaration in the context of the legislative process would be an appropriate remedy, and that recognizing a constitutional obligation to consult would allow the court to shape the legal framework while respecting the constitutional role of the legislative branch of government.

Why It Matters

Mikisew represents a missed opportunity. Rather than causing disruption and chaos, a decision that the duty to consult applies to legislative development could have set the stage for respectful engagement with Indigenous Peoples about the development of laws, and in turn avoided a multitude of potential legal challenges to legislation that affects Aboriginal rights and treaty rights.

Unlike other jurisdictions (e.g. New Zealand), Indigenous Peoples in Canada have no direct, separate involvement in the development of legislation. *Mikisew* could have addressed this issue, in part, by affirming a positive obligation on government to consider and substantially address the concerns of Indigenous Peoples while legislation is being developed.

Importantly, it would be an error for federal and provincial governments to assume that based on *Mikisew*, they can ignore the rights and interests of Indigenous Peoples when drafting legislation. The reasons of both the majority and dissenting judges in *Mikisew* provide strong, clear affirmation that the Crown should engage directly with Indigenous Peoples, both in order to fulfill its obligation to act honourably and to avoid the prospect of future litigation in respect of legislation that infringes the rights of Indigenous Peoples.

While the entire court in *Mikisew* identified different opportunities for Indigenous Peoples to challenge federal and provincial legislation that affects their constitutional rights, at the end of the day the decision underscores the need for a new path forward. Indigenous Peoples should not be forced to fight for a place at the table in the development of the colonizers' laws. Real reconciliation requires recognition of Indigenous Peoples' inherent law-making authority and its place within Canada's constitutional order.

Saving the Specific Claims Tribunal:
Williams Lake Indian Band v. Canada (2018)

There are two general categories of negotiated claims in Canada: comprehensive claims that include Aboriginal title, rights and self-government; and specific claims, which are based on specific historical wrongs done to First Nations.

Background on Specific Claims

In the 1980s the federal government acknowledged its long history of failing to protect Indigenous Peoples' interests, especially in relation to reserve lands, and that it was unfair that these historical wrongs remained unresolved because of the operation of limitation periods in Canadian law. Consequently, the federal specific claims process was created. It allows First Nations to file historical claims with the federal government in the hope that Canada will acknowledge an outstanding lawful obligation and negotiate a settlement.

Instead of resolving historical wrongs, the specific claims process spread resentment and cynicism. First Nations worked hard to research and file hundreds of claims that disappeared into a black hole of the federal government's making. After half-hearted and ineffectual efforts to reform the specific claims process, in 2008 the federal government passed legislation creating the Specific Claims Tribunal, an independent administrative tribunal made up of superior court judges responsible for making final, binding decisions on the validity of specific claims and the amount of compensation owed First Nations. While there is no appeal of the tribunal's decisions, the legislation allows for judicial reviews to the Federal Court of Appeal.

What It's About

The Colony of British Columbia was founded in 1858 on the unlawful premise that the British Crown owned Indigenous lands and had the right to give away these lands to so-called settlers. The first step for a settler in acquiring title to Indigenous lands was to file a pre-emption. While most Indigenous land was up for grabs, as far as settlers were concerned, an exception under colonial law and policy was that settlers could not pre-empt occupied Indigenous village sites. This prohibition was routinely ignored by settlers and government officials.

When British Columbia became part of Canada in 1871, the federal government assumed responsibility for creating Indian reserves and the Province of British Columbia agreed to transfer Crown lands as required. This arrangement led to the federal and provincial governments' creation of the Joint Indian Reserve Commission which, through the 1870s and 1880s, travelled the province investigating the status of Indian reserves. As part of the commission's work, it came to light that the village site of Williams Lake Indian Band (WLIB) on the shores of Williams Lake had been pre-empted beginning in the 1860s. Instead of insisting that the Province cancel the pre-emption, the federal government acquired different lands for the WLIB's reserve.

Soon after the Specific Claims Tribunal opened for business in 2008, WLIB filed a claim to its lost village site. The tribunal eventually decided in favour of WLIB. The federal government took the case to the Federal Court of Appeal, which set aside the tribunal's decision and dismissed the First Nation's claim. WLIB appealed to the Supreme Court. The Supreme Court zeroed in on two issues: How much, if any, deference was owed to the new Tribunal by a court reviewing one of its decisions? And did the federal government, by operation of the Specific Claims Tribunal Act, assume liability for the colonial government's failure to protect the village site?

On the first issue, the court held that the tribunal is owed a high degree of deference. The tribunal is made up of specialized superior court judges responsible for assessing claims steeped in the complexities of fiduciary law and based on complicated and nuanced historical facts. The court concluded that the tribunal has a distinctive task requiring significant flexibility. Consequently, a reviewing court must show the tribunal significant deference when reviewing one of its decisions.

The second issue—whether the federal government was liable for the colonial government's failure to protect the lands from pre-emption—was hotly debated by the court. The majority of justices, five, concluded that in this case Canada was liable and while the tribunal could have provided better reasons, its decision should be restored.

In separate reasons, two of the justices agreed with the majority for the most part, but would have sent the matter back to the tribunal to provide a more detailed explanation as to how the federal government was liable for the wrong of the colony. A further two justices dissented from the majority's decision and questioned both whether the federal government had breached its fiduciary duty to WLIB and whether it could have inherited responsibility for the colonial government's failure to protect the village site.

In the end, the tribunal's decision validating WLIB's claim was restored. The court directed the tribunal to proceed to phase two of the hearing, which would decide how much compensation was owed WLIB for loss of the village site and how the compensation should be apportioned between the federal and provincial governments. Importantly, WLIB may not be able to recover any money owed by the Province because an award by the tribunal is not enforceable against the Province. Following the court's decision, the parties agreed to enter into negotiations to settle the claim.

The court's decision is hugely important, not only for First Nations in British Columbia but for the entire country. There are numerous similar "village site" claims in British Columbia based on the colonial government's failure to enforce its own laws and the federal government's failure, after confederation, to protect First Nations' interests in their lands. These claims, and potentially other claims dating from the colonial period, can now move forward both in the specific claims process and, if need be, at the Specific Claims Tribunal.

Outside of British Columbia, the decision is powerful support for arguments based on the indivisibility of the Crown's fiduciary obligations to First Nations and the Crown's obligation to protect specific Indigenous lands. While the decision is informed by British Columbia's unique reserve creation process, it will likely play a prominent role in helping settle similar outstanding questions across the country and embolden First Nations to pursue their own claims from the colonial period.

Ultimately the decision is most important for saving the Specific Claims Tribunal. By not only disagreeing with the tribunal, but also by paying it so little regard as to decide the matter itself, the Federal Court of Appeal undercut the tribunal's authority, processes and integrity. Had the Supreme Court upheld the Federal Court of Appeal's decision, First Nations would have abandoned the tribunal process en masse. The court's support for the important work of the tribunal and its conclusion that the tribunal's decisions are owed a high degree of deference has breathed new life into the tribunal. It has restored First Nations' confidence in the tribunal's processes and rekindled hope that the tribunal will deliver justice to hundreds of First Nations across the country.

Treaties at Risk: The Fort McKay First Nation

With Kate Gunn

Despite decades of strong Indigenous voices demanding that governments honour the treaties, and numerous court decisions supporting their calls for action, governments across Canada continue to disrespect and ignore their treaty obligations. In *Fort McKay First Nation v. Prosper Petroleum Ltd.* (2020), the Alberta Court of Appeal has become the most recent Canadian court to highlight the disconnect between governments' legal obligations to treaty peoples and their shameful and continuing disregard for the treaty relationship.

In 1899, predecessors of Fort McKay First Nation entered into Treaty 8 with the Crown. The Treaty was intended to establish a relationship of mutual respect and benefit, and to set the terms by which the Indigenous signatories to Treaty 8 would peacefully share their territory while preserving their own way of life.

In recent decades, lands surrounding Fort McKay have been subject to extensive oil sands development. In 2003, Fort McKay and the Government of Alberta entered into negotiations to develop a plan to address the cumulative effects of industrial activities on Fort McKay's treaty rights in the Moose Lake area. The Province promised, as part of the negotiations, to protect lands in the Moose Lake area from further development.

In 2018, before the plan to protect lands in the Moose Lake area was finalized, the Alberta Energy Regulator (AER) approved an application for a bitumen recovery project near Fort McKay's reserves. Fort McKay appealed the AER's decision on the basis that the AER failed to consider the honour of the Crown and should have delayed approval of the project until Fort McKay's negotiations with the Province were completed.

The Court of Appeal allowed the appeal and ordered the AER to reconsider whether the project was in the public interest, taking into account the honour of the Crown and commitments made by Alberta in the course of an ongoing negotiation process with Fort McKay. The court held that the honour of the Crown requires governments to act in a way that accomplishes the intended purposes of the treaty, and that this overarching obligation may give rise to duties beyond consultation, including the requirement to keep promises made in negotiations to protect treaty rights.

The court acknowledged that the reality of extensive industrial development may make it increasingly difficult for the Province to keep certain treaty promises, including the right to hunt. However, the court emphasized that the Province remains under an ongoing obligation to honourably implement the treaty, including by taking into account the cumulative effects of development on treaty rights.

The court further held that where a regulatory agency such as the AER is required to consider whether a project is in the public interest, it must ensure that its decision is consistent with section 35 of the 1982 Constitution Act. In this case, the AER failed to fulfill its responsibility to consider the honour of the Crown and potential impacts of a project on Aboriginal and treaty rights as part of fulfilling its public interest mandate.

Why It Matters

The importance of the numbered treaties and the Crown's corresponding obligations have been repeatedly and unequivocally confirmed by the Supreme Court for many years. As the court held in *Mikisew* (2005), the honour of the Crown is at stake in the performance of every treaty obligation. The treaty relationship mandates an ongoing process whereby the Crown, acting honourably, must ensure that treaty rights remain protected in the face of industrial development. Too often, however, Indigenous Peoples' treaty rights have been sidelined where large-scale resource projects are at stake. This is particularly true in Alberta, where oil sands development has left Fort McKay and other First Nations unable to use large portions of their lands.

The Alberta Court of Appeal's decision is an important reminder to Alberta and other provinces that the Crown's treaty promises are to be taken seriously. The honour of the Crown requires that it take steps to protect a First Nation's treaty rights long before those rights are infringed. This includes taking into account the cumulative effects of resource development and promises made in the course of modern-day negotiations. Government decisions that fail to consider the impacts of a project on a First Nation's treaty rights cannot be in the public interest.

It is a telling comment on the Alberta government's systemic failure to live up to its treaty obligations that it was necessary for the Court of Appeal to remind the Province of its treaty obligations. Will Alberta and other provinces finally begin to take their treaty obligations seriously? Only time will tell. Importantly, the *Fort McKay* decision makes clear that courts are prepared to enforce the Crown's obligations in respect of treaty implementation. Alberta needs to accept the fact that disrespecting the treaties is contrary to Canadian law and bad policy. The possibility of cancelled projects creates uncertainty for everyone. Certainty, and honour, can only be realized through fulfilling treaty obligations.

A Pipeline Too Far: The Problem with the Duty to Consult

Despite a wealth of smarts and determination, to date Indigenous people have not been able to stop the twinning of the Trans Mountain pipeline. Ever since the 2004 *Haida Nation* decision, the duty to consult and accommodate has proven a powerful tool in the struggle for greater respect for Aboriginal rights and title. Courts have handed Indigenous Peoples numerous significant victories—they have also created a blueprint for overriding Indigenous Peoples' inherent and constitutional rights.

The courts' decisions about the Enbridge and Trans Mountain pipelines exemplify the problem with the duty to consult. In 2016 the Federal Court of Appeal quashed the decisions authorizing the Enbridge pipeline. At the same time, it provided the federal government with a recipe for approving it—discuss new information with First Nations, consider further conditions and provide reasons for its decision. Similarly, in 2018 the Federal Court of Appeal stopped the Trans Mountain pipeline from proceeding. Again, it outlined the shortcomings in the consultations that had been carried out so far and supplied the federal government with a checklist for the further consultation that was required. For political reasons, the federal government decided not to have a second go at having the Enbridge pipeline approved. In contrast, it did follow the court's requirements for further consultation on the Trans Mountain pipeline and unsurprisingly, eventually succeeded in winning the court's stamp of approval.

The court's decisions on Enbridge and Trans Mountain underscore the limitations of the duty to consult and accommodate as the basis for reconciliation. All too often, the courts' message to government has been that as long as you follow the script and your decision is within the realm of possible outcomes, we'll defer to your decision.

The legal challenges to the Trans Mountain pipeline created an opportunity for a different ending. It was an opportunity for the court to acknowledge the duty to consult's downward spiral toward procedural oblivion and to take a stand in the name of recognition and respect. There were two basic elements to stopping the Trans Mountain pipeline. First, the court had to acknowledge the obvious. The pipeline will exponentially increase tanker traffic through the Salish Sea. The risk of an oil spill will increase.

However remote the possibility, a major spill will have catastrophic effects on the Indigenous Peoples of the Salish Sea. A major spill runs the risk of extinguishing the very basis for their recognition as distinct Aboriginal peoples under the constitution.

Second, the court would have had to acknowledge that in some cases deference, procedural consultation and a "balancing of interests" simply will not do. The very core of Indigenous Peoples' identity as distinct nations protected by section 35 of the constitution is at stake. There is a limit to government's authority to endanger the continued existence of Indigenous Peoples. There is a line that cannot be crossed. The Supreme Court confirmed the underlying principle in 1997 in *Delgamuukw* and restated it in 2014 in *Tsilhqot'in*. The importance of an Aboriginal right combined with the potential serious impact of the government decision on that right creates circumstances where a project cannot proceed without Indigenous consent. A project that would destroy an Indigenous People's identity requires more than consultation. Such a project cannot be countenanced because it would breach the Crown's fiduciary obligations to Aboriginal people and the fundamental promise of section 35 to protect and perpetuate distinct Aboriginal peoples into the future and forever.

The Trans Mountain pipeline can still be stopped but doing so requires an act of affirmation. Despite the court decisions to date, it is open to the federal government to affirm that while constitutional rights may not be absolute, the promise of section 35 is inviolate. There are interests that cannot be balanced, risks that cannot be mitigated and lines that cannot be crossed—there are promises that cannot be broken.

Reconciliation at the End of a Gun:
The Wet'suwet'en and the RCMP

I spend a lot of time in small towns across Canada. Often, I go for lunch with my First Nations clients. With one of my clients I noticed that we always ate at the same local restaurant over and over again, despite there being what seemed to be several other perfectly good places to eat. When I finally suggested we try one of those restaurants for a change, the response from my clients jarred me out of my comfortable complacency: *This is where we feel safe*, they said.

The threat and reality of violence is at the core of Indigenous experiences with non-Indigenous Canada. My clients live with the threat of violence their entire lives. Violence inflicted on them and their loved ones by non-Indigenous people.

From an early age, they learn the cruel reality that being a visibly identifiable Indigenous person in Canada means they live with a heightened risk of being insulted, attacked and killed by non-Indigenous people.

From Colten Boushie to Tina Fontaine to a grandfather and his granddaughter handcuffed outside a bank in downtown Vancouver, violence against Indigenous people is the Canadian reality.

It is a violence that extends beyond the personal. It has been an ever-present tool in the colonization and continuing oppression and displacement of Indigenous people in Canada. From Indigenous perspectives, Canadian history is a horror show of violence. From Governor Cornwallis' bounty on Mi'kmaw scalps, to military attacks on the fledgling Métis Nation, to Louis Riel hanged in Regina, to John A. Macdonald's policy of starvation of the Plains Cree, to Poundmaker's imprisonment, to the hanging of Tsilhqot'in Chiefs, to residential schools and the sixties scoop, the list goes on and on.

Importantly, Canadian state-sanctioned violence against Indigenous people is not simply a matter of history and easy apologies. It is a modern-day reality. Think back over the last twenty years: Oka, Gustafsen Lake, Ipperwash, Burnt Church, Elsipogtog, Unist'ot'en.

On February 6, 2020, my Wet'suwet'en clients in Northern British Columbia again faced the reality of what it too often means to be an Indigenous person in Canada. While Wet'suwet'en Hereditary Chiefs and their supporters seek to defend their land against a multinational pipeline company and a provincial government that appears to believe reconciliation occurs at the end of a gun, the RCMP again amassed an armed force in an attempt to overwhelm and subdue them.

In preparation for a similar military-style raid against my clients last year, the RCMP employed a strategy of "lethal overwatch" and using as much violence as they deemed necessary to "sterilize the site."

This time around, the RCMP assured Canadians that the police officers tasked with dismantling Wet'suwet'en camps, handcuffing unarmed land protectors and marching them off to jail had first undergone cultural awareness training.

For many Indigenous people the very language of "peace, order and good government" is infused with and inseparable from real, visceral, frightening experiences of violence.

On a blustery day in Northern Ontario, over a hundred miles from the nearest road, I informed Anishinaabe clients that the provincial government was finally willing to sit down and explore avenues for them to exercise their inherent Indigenous "jurisdiction."

The Elders politely smiled, turned away and spoke among themselves in Oji-Cree. After a few minutes, as often happens, I was told a story.

It was a story about being a child and wanting to visit cousins in the neighbouring community downriver. Of travelling in an open boat, of rounding a bend in the river and seeing cousins handcuffed to poplar trees.

For my clients, the word *jurisdiction* didn't connote fairness, justice and the rule of law. It conjured visions of the personifications of government and institutional authority, the priest, the RCMP officer, the Indian Agent—the people who handcuffed their cousins to poplar trees.

The threat and reality of violence extends beyond language—it has become part of the built environment that contains and defines our daily experiences.

I grew up in rural Manitoba on the fringes of the Peguis First Nation reserve. My mother held a wide variety of jobs. I thought she could do anything. I still do. One of her jobs was working in the beer parlour in the hotel in a nearby small town.

Occasionally, after school I'd wait at the hotel until her shift ended. Hoping to get a few dollars to buy a serving of french fries in the adjoining diner, I'd grip the counter at the off-sales window, pull myself up and look into the beer parlour, straining to get my mom's attention as she served draft beer and punched out change from the coin belt around her waist.

The room was dingy with a dirty carpet soaked in cheap beer. A low steel fence ran down the middle of the room, dividing it in two. I asked my mom, "Why is there a fence?" Her answer brought many of my childhood experiences into focus: "It's to separate the Indians from the white guys." Any Indigenous person daring to sit on the wrong side of that fence risked a severe beating.

When I hear the word *reconciliation* I think of that fence. I think of how it represents Canada's long history of segregating Indigenous people and perpetuating violence against them.

Violence towards Indigenous people, personal, institutional and state-sanctioned, is woven into the very fabric of Canadian life, both its history and its present. It is in the words we speak and the buildings and cities we inhabit. Canadian law sanctions it, politicians justify it, industry profits from it, the public turns a blind eye.

With the RCMP raid on the Wet'suwet'en, violence has also become the hallmark of reconciliation.

The Wet'suwet'en, Aboriginal Title and the Rule of Law: An Explainer

With Kate Gunn

The RCMP's enforcement of the Coastal GasLink injunction against the Wet'suwet'en has ignited a national debate about the law and the rights of Indigenous people.

Unfortunately, misconceptions and conflicting information threaten to derail this important conversation. Below, we attempt to provide clear, straightforward answers to address some of these fundamental misunderstandings.

What about support for the project from the Wet'suwet'en elected chiefs and councils?

Media outlets across the country have repeatedly reported that First Nations along the pipeline route, including the Wet'suwet'en, have signed agreements in support of the project. Underlying this statement are several key issues that require clarification.

First, the Wet'suwet'en, like many Indigenous groups in Canada, are governed by both a traditional governance system and elected chiefs and councils. The chief and council system exists under the Indian Act, a piece of federal legislation. It was introduced by the federal government in the nineteenth century as one of Canada's attempts to systematically oppress and displace Indigenous law and governance.

The Wet'suwet'en hereditary governance system predates colonization and continues to exist today. The Wet'suwet'en and Gitxsan Hereditary Chiefs, not the Indian Act chiefs and councils, were the plaintiffs in the landmark *Delgamuukw–Gisday'way* Aboriginal title case. They provided the court with exhaustive and detailed evidence of the Wet'suwet'en and Gitxsan governance system and the legal authority of Hereditary Chiefs.

Unless otherwise authorized by the Indigenous Nation members, the authority of elected chiefs and councils is limited to the powers set out under the Indian Act. The Indian Act does not provide authority for a chief and council to make decisions about lands beyond the boundaries of the First Nation's reserves.

By contrast, the Hereditary Chiefs are responsible under Wet'suwet'en law and governance for making decisions relating to their ancestral lands. It is these lands that the Hereditary Chiefs are seeking to protect from the impacts of the pipeline project, not Indian Act reserve lands.

Second, Indigenous Peoples hold rights to lands in Canada that extend far beyond the boundaries of Indian Act reserves, including Aboriginal title and rights to the lands they used and occupied prior to the arrival of Europeans and the assertion of Crown sovereignty. Aboriginal title and rights are protected under the 1982 Constitution Act—the highest law in Canada's legal system.

Third, the fact that First Nations have signed agreements

with Coastal GasLink does not in itself mean that its members support the project without qualification. Across the country, Indian Act band councils are forced to make difficult choices about how to provide for their members—a situation that exists in large part due to the process of colonization, chronic underfunding for reserve infrastructure, and refusal on the part of the Crown to meaningfully recognize Indigenous rights and jurisdiction. The fact that elected Wet'suwet'en chiefs and councils have entered into benefit agreements with Coastal GasLink should not be taken as unconditional support for the project.

Finally, similar to how Canada functions as a confederation with separate provinces with their own authority, First Nation decisions on major projects are not simply a matter of majority rules. The Quebec provincial government made it clear that it was opposed to and would not sanction the proposed Energy East pipeline. The federal government and other provincial governments respected Quebec's right to make this decision. Similarly, First Nations often disagree about major projects. One cannot speak for another and the majority cannot simply overrule the minority or individual First Nations.

But aren't the Indian Act chiefs and councils democratically elected?

Chiefs and councils under the Indian Act may be elected, but they do not necessarily speak for the nation as a whole. Most chiefs and councils are elected by status "Indians" whose names are on an Indian Act band list. The federal government decides who is entitled to be registered as a status Indian through the registration provisions of the Indian Act. The registration provisions are restrictive and have been subject to numerous legal challenges.

Some Indian Act bands have adopted custom election codes that allow non-status Indians to vote. However, in general if an individual does not meet the criteria for "Indian" status under the Indian Act, they will not be able to vote in band elections.

Critically, the fact that an Indigenous person is not registered under the Indian Act does not mean they are not part of the wider collective that holds Aboriginal title and rights. The Indigenous collective that holds Aboriginal title and rights is not limited to status Indians registered under the Indian Act.

But what about the "rule of law"?

Land law in Canada is much more complicated and uncertain than most non-Indigenous Canadians appreciate. When European colonizers arrived, numerous Indigenous nations existed throughout the land we now call Canada. Each Indigenous nation, including the Wet'suwet'en, had their own unique and specific set of land laws. Canadian courts continue to recognize that Indigenous laws form part of Canada's legal system, including as a basis for Aboriginal title. The "rule of law" therefore includes both Canadian and Indigenous law.

Under international and British law at the time of colonization, unless Indigenous people were conquered or treaties were made with them, the Indigenous interest in their land was to be respected by the law of the European colonizing nation. The British Crown never conquered or made a treaty with the Wet'suwet'en.

In the early days of the colonization of what is now British Columbia, the British government was well aware that based on its own laws it was highly questionable that it had any right to occupy Indigenous lands or assign rights in those lands to individuals or companies.

Nonetheless, beginning in the 1860s the colony of British Columbia began passing its own land laws and giving out property interests in Indigenous land without any established legal right to do so. The source of the Province's authority over Indigenous lands remains unresolved in Canadian law today. In 2004 the Supreme Court of Canada referred to the historical and current situation as British Columbia's de facto control of Indigenous lands and resources.

In other words, the Supreme Court recognized that the Province's authority to issue permits for Indigenous lands, including the type of permits issued for the Coastal Gas-Link pipeline, is not based on established legal authority. It is based on the fact that the Province has proceeded, for over one hundred fifty years, to make unilateral decisions about Indigenous lands.

The fact that the Province has acted since the 1860s as though it has full authority to decide how Indigenous Peoples' lands are used does not make doing so legal or just.

Isn't this Crown land?

Under Canadian law, the Crown, as represented by the various provincial governments, has what is referred to as the underlying interest in all land within provincial boundaries. This is based on the discredited and internationally repudiated Doctrine of Discovery. Courts in Canada have concluded that regardless of the Doctrine of Discovery having been rejected around the world, they are unable to question its legitimacy.

Importantly, even if one accepts that provincial governments hold the underlying interest in "Crown land," that interest is subject to strict limits. It does not mean that the provincial governments have a legal right to occupy Indigenous lands or to grant rights to those lands to individuals or companies. Nor does it give provincial governments the right to sell Indigenous land, assign interests to people or companies or forcibly remove Indigenous people from their territories.

The right to benefit from the land, decide how the land should be used, and exclude other people from entering on or using the land is separate from the Crown's underlying interest in the land. The right to benefit from the land and exclude others from using the land is part of what Canadian courts have described as Aboriginal title. Aboriginal title, including Wet'suwet'en Aboriginal title, takes precedence over the Crown's underlying interest in the land.

While Canadian courts have held that provincial governments may be able to infringe Aboriginal title, the requirements to justify infringement are onerous. The provincial government has not attempted to justify its infringement of Wet'suwet'en Aboriginal title.

But what about the Wet'suwet'en not having proven their Aboriginal title in court?

As with other Indigenous nations, Wet'suwet'en Aboriginal title exists as a matter of law. It predates the colony of British Columbia and British Columbia's entry into confederation in 1871. Its existence was not created by section 35 of the 1982 Constitution Act, nor does it depend on recognition by Canadian courts. Canadian courts can recognize Wet'suwet'en Aboriginal title, but they cannot create it. A court declaration of Aboriginal title would merely confirm its existence under Canadian law.

In the *Delgamuukw–Gisday'way* case, the courts heard extensive evidence about Wet'suwet'en title and rights. Ultimately, the Supreme Court refused to issue a declaration in favour of the Wet'suwet'en because of a technicality in the pleadings. The parties were left to either negotiate a resolution or begin a new trial.

Regardless of whether there is a court declaration, it is open to the Province to recognize and respect the existence of Wet'suwet'en title at any time. Instead of recognizing the existence of Aboriginal title, the current provincial government continues to adhere to a policy of denial. This is the same policy endorsed by every provincial government since British Columbia became a part of Canada.

As long as it maintains this policy, the Province avoids the implications of having to recognize Wet'suwet'en title and fulfill its corresponding obligations under Canadian law. By its continued denial of Wet'suwet'en title, the Province avoids the hard work of reconciling its longstanding failure to respect Indigenous land rights with the continued existence and resurgence of Wet'suwet'en law and governance.

The Wet'suwet'en, Governments and Indigenous Peoples: A Five-Step Plan for Reconciliation

Canada has reached a watershed moment.

Will it continue to bulldoze Indigenous rights in the name of resource exploitation and jobs and profits for the few, or will it renounce its colonialist past and strike out on the path of respect, collaboration and partnership with Indigenous people?

Using the current national response to the Wet'suwet'en controversy as a springboard for discussion, here's my five-step plan for preparing the ground for real reconciliation.

1. Renounce violence against Indigenous people

Canada must stop using the threat and reality of state-sanctioned violence to forcibly remove Indigenous people from their land. Reconciliation cannot be achieved through force.

The threat of violence as a tool of oppression of Indigenous people raises the spectre of Canada's long, violent history of colonialism. A post-colonial world does not include violence.

True reconciliation cannot begin until state-sanctioned violence is no longer an option.

2. Implement UNDRIP

We would not be in the situation we are in today if the British Columbia government was serious about implementing the United Nations Declaration on the Rights of Indigenous Peoples.

In late 2019, the Declaration on the Rights of Indigenous Peoples Act became law in British Columbia to great fanfare. Instead of marking a new day for reconciliation and respect, it has fostered resentment and cynicism.

Why? Because in response to the Wet'suwet'en standoff, the provincial government failed to respect its own law. It took the position that its UNDRIP legislation does not apply to projects that had already received provincial approval. Its position is indefensible.

British Columbia's UNDRIP legislation is not simply forward-looking. It imposes a positive obligation on the provincial government to ensure that UNDRIP principles are implemented in the ongoing application of existing provincial law. In this context, *law* includes legislation, regulations and policies.

The federal government is currently planning to introduce its own UNDRIP legislation. It must not repeat British Columbia's mistake.

3. Fulfill the federal government's role

Until the last few days, the federal government has been sadly absent as the RCMP invaded Wet'suwet'en land and demonstrations of support erupted across the country.

The federal government has an important constitutional role to play when Indigenous Peoples find their rights threatened by provincial governments and resource extraction companies.

When Canada came into being in 1867, the federal government was assigned exclusive legislative authority over "Indians and Lands reserved for Indians." This was done for two main reasons: ensure a national policy on Indigenous issues and protect Indigenous Peoples from what at the time were referred to as "local settler majorities"—we now call them provincial governments.

In recent years, the Supreme Court has expanded the role of provincial governments in resolving disagreements over Aboriginal and treaty rights. This change does not absolve the federal government of its continuing responsibilities. Because it does not face the same local pressure to remove Indigenous people from their land as provincial governments do, the federal government has an important role to play in resolving disputes.

The federal government must have the courage to fulfill its historical and legal responsibilities to Indigenous Peoples.

4. Sign recognition agreements

Recognition is the prerequisite for reconciliation.

Today's controversy is the result of and a continuation of British Columbia's hundred-fifty-year history of denying Indigenous rights, including Aboriginal title. While the current provincial government publicly talks of recognition and reconciliation, in the courts and all too often on the ground, it perpetuates British Columbia's long history of denial.

Because provincial and federal governments continue to deny the existence of Aboriginal title, the courts hold them to no more than the procedural requirements to consult and, in some cases, accommodate. As the recent Trans Mountain pipeline decision from the Federal Court of Appeal demonstrated, the duty to consult has become an ineffectual tool for Indigenous Peoples seeking to protect their Aboriginal title lands.

Instead of creating the basis for meaningful dialogue, the duty to consult has too often become the gateway to the RCMP's militarized enforcement of injunctions against Indigenous people. Over fifteen years ago, the Supreme Court recognized that injunctions are all-or-nothing solutions with Indigenous people too often finding themselves on the losing end.

It is open to the federal and provincial governments to jettison denial policies and recognize Aboriginal title through agreement. As the Supreme Court has repeatedly reminded all parties, the courts are not required to be involved. While Indigenous rights exist without government recognition, a formal recognition agreement would put an end to the destructive status quo of denial.

If there are issues about so-called overlaps with neighbouring Indigenous Peoples, initial agreements can either be limited to core Aboriginal title lands or acknowledge the necessity of resolving competing claims for title. After a recognition agreement is signed, the hard work of creating the space for respecting Aboriginal title through subsequent implementation agreements can begin.

Fortunately, we have clear evidence that the sky does not fall and the economy does not grind to a halt when Aboriginal title is recognized. In 2014 the Tsilhqot'in obtained a declaration of Aboriginal title to a portion of their territory. What have they been doing since? They've been in serious, respectful negotiations with the provincial and federal governments based on the recognized existence of their Aboriginal title.

A final, but crucial aspect of any potential recognition agreement would be that it would confirm respect for Indigenous law. One of the most concerning developments in the dispute between the Wet'suwet'en and the pipeline company is that in its most recent injunction decision the BC Supreme Court held that while Indigenous law exists, it cannot be put into effect as part of Canadian law without a treaty, legislation or agreement.

While there are serious questions to be asked about the soundness of the court's conclusion, its immediate effect has been to undermine many Indigenous Peoples' confidence in the Canadian legal system. A recognition agreement that recognized both Aboriginal title and Indigenous law would go a long way to renewing Indigenous Peoples' confidence in Canadian courts.

5. Embrace consent-based decision-making

Certainty, respect and collaboration depend on consent-based decision-making. As long as governments continue to raise the fear of an Indigenous veto, they will fail Indigenous people and the wider public.

As many commentators have noted, veto and consent are not the same thing—the former is exercised arbitrarily, the latter is actively sought and occasionally withheld. When government and industry talk of "no veto," the implication is "therefore we're going to do what we want to do whether you support it or not." This is the antithesis of good faith consultation. It results in projects being forced through over valid Indigenous concerns and possible alternatives.

Case in point, several years ago the Wet'suwet'en Hereditary Chiefs proposed an alternative route for the Coastal GasLink project, a route that would traverse a portion of their territory already developed for industry and that would avoid a pristine, undeveloped part of their territory. The company rejected the chiefs' proposed alternative route based on technical issues and additional cost.

Across Canada, alternative solutions proposed by Indigenous people can be rejected with confidence because federal and provincial governments emphasize the lack of an Indigenous veto instead of seeking consent. As long as governments rely on the language of veto, there is little incentive to work with Indigenous Peoples to find respectful, workable solutions.

Consent-based decision-making is about actively engaging with Indigenous people with the intention of identifying solutions that will result in Indigenous consent. It includes accepting that in certain situations, the answer is going to be no. Non-Indigenous governments always retain the right to reject a project. Indigenous Peoples deserve the same respect.

In Canada the consent principle dates at least as far back as the Royal Proclamation of 1763. The Supreme Court has identified it as the preferable path of engagement and as a necessity in certain circumstances.

The question arises—who is authorized to give consent? Indigenous Peoples across the country are working to revitalize their Indigenous laws and governance, either separate from or working with the existing Indian Act chief and council system. The federal and provincial governments need to support and respect this work.

Consent-based decision-making is practical and workable. It respects Indigenous Peoples' right to make decisions about how their land will or will not be used. A commitment to consent-based decision-making will create certainty for all Canadians.

Which Way, Canada?

The voices of the status quo are loud and relentless. Hiding behind the self-serving rhetoric of the "rule of law" and the "public interest," they call for the removal of Indigenous Peoples from their lands.

Canadians have a choice to make. Will they double down on denial and oppression or will they embrace respect for constitutional rights and Indigenous Peoples' laws? Our children will judge the choice we make today.

Consent Is Not a Four-Letter Word: What Next for the Trans Mountain Pipeline?

In 1603, on his first voyage to North America, Samuel de Champlain sailed down the St. Lawrence and anchored his ship at the mouth of the Saguenay River, northeast of modern-day Quebec City. Champlain was eager to explore the upper reaches of the Saguenay to establish valuable trade relations. He also hoped to discover a route to the fabled Northwest Passage—but it was not to be. This was Innu territory. Without the consent of the Innu, Champlain could not pass up the Saguenay, and Innu consent was not given.

Over four centuries later, Champlain's encounter with the Innu echoed across the Canadian landscape. On October 3, 2018, the federal government enlisted former Supreme Court Justice Frank Iacobucci to salvage its failed consultations with Indigenous Peoples over the Trans Mountain pipeline. While Mr. Iacobucci would no doubt provide excellent advice, the early signs from the federal government were not encouraging. According to Fisheries and Oceans Minister Jonathan Wilkinson, the federal government's primary obligation is not to address Indigenous concerns—it's to satisfy the courts.

All Canadians would be well served if Minister Wilkinson and his cabinet colleagues had considered the significance of Champlain's 1603 encounter with the Innu. During the early

years of the European encounter with the Indigenous Peoples
of North America, the French prided themselves on their
comparatively positive relations with Indigenous Peoples,
many of whom became their allies against the British. In large
part this relationship was grounded on recognition of the
fact that the French were visitors in Indigenous territories. If
they wanted to maintain their position, they had to respect
Indigenous authority.

Following Champlain's first voyage, relationships with
Indigenous Peoples based on recognition, respect and consent
were repeated as Europeans moved across the continent from
east, west, north and south. It was only after the devastating
toll of European diseases and Canada's genocidal practices on
Indigenous people that colonizers were able to systematically
disregard the requirement for Indigenous consent.

The principle of consent is also well established in international and Canadian law. The United Nations Declaration
on the Rights of Indigenous Peoples (UNDRIP) has enshrined
consent as the international standard. In the sixth of its
ten principles respecting its relationship with Indigenous
Peoples, the federal government has endorsed consent-based
processes.

In law, the recognition of the requirement for Indigenous
consent dates at least as far back as the Royal Proclamation
of 1763. More recently, the Supreme Court of Canada in the
Delgamuukw, Tsilhqot'in and *Ktunaxa* decisions has discussed
when, under Canadian law, Indigenous consent is either
required or at the very least is the preferred course of action.

Unfortunately, consent has been confused with *veto*, the
favourite word of all who seek to marginalize and undermine

Indigenous Peoples. In the context of Aboriginal law in Canada, *veto* refers to sitting on the sidelines and jumping up at the end of the process to arbitrarily play a trump card to stop a proposed project. Consent is something different.

Consent is grounded on two important words: recognition and respect. Recognition and respect for the historical and legal fact that despite having undergone centuries of colonization and genocide, Indigenous Peoples have never relinquished their right and responsibility to make decisions about their lands.

Anyone proposing to enter onto or do something with Indigenous Peoples' lands and waters should approach them with an open heart and an open mind and seek their consent. Doing so will set the foundation for the meaningful dialogue and process of give-and-take that the federal government neglected during its failed first attempt to consult on the Trans Mountain pipeline.

Whether or not the Trans Mountain pipeline will ever be built is uncertain. What is certain is that until federal and provincial governments abandon the low road of minimalist consultation and stop trying to silence Indigenous people by shouting "No veto!" they will continue to sow discord, opposition and distrust. Indigenous Peoples are offering them a better way forward—they should take it.

Addendum

In 2018, the Federal Court of Appeal quashed the federal government's approval of the Trans Mountain pipeline based on its failure to fulfill its duty to consult Indigenous Peoples

(Tsleil-Waututh Nation v. Canada (Attorney General), 2018 FCA 153). As predicted, the pipeline was reapproved following further consultation. The Federal Court of Appeal dismissed First Nations' legal challenges to this second approval in 2020 (*Coldwater First Nation v. Canada (Attorney General)*, 2020 FCA 34).

A Monument to Racism: BC Doubles Down on Site C Dam

With Kate Gunn

To acknowledge British Columbia's one hundred fiftieth anniversary as a province, the University of Victoria and the Canadian Centre for Policy Alternatives released an open-source publication entitled *Challenging Racist "British Columbia": 150 Years and Counting.* A few days later, the BC government announced it would proceed with the Site C dam, the Province's monument to its historic and continuing policy of racism toward Indigenous Peoples.

The Site C dam builds on and perpetuates BC's history of sacrificing Indigenous lands for short-term profit. In the 1960s, flush with American dollars paid to it for allowing the construction of dams on the Columbia River and the flooding of the lands of the Ktunaxa, *Syilx* Okanagan and Secwepemc, BC built the massive W.A.C. Bennett Dam on the Peace River in Treaty 8. Upstream, the Williston Reservoir flooded the lands of Treaty 8 First Nations in BC, destroying their economies and undermining their cultures and communities. Downstream, the dam interrupted the natural water flows of the Peace River, endangering the livelihoods of Treaty 8 First Nations in Alberta. The dam continues to threaten the Peace–Athabasca Delta, the largest freshwater inland delta in North America and a designated UNESCO World Heritage site.

The Site C dam capitalizes on the destruction of Treaty 8 territory and the ongoing infringement of treaty rights. It will also cause additional, irreversible impacts on the lands and rights of Indigenous Peoples in Treaty 8 on both sides of the Alberta–BC border.

In July 2020, the BC government revealed there were significant structural problems with the foundation of the Site C dam. The Province commissioned a series of expert reports to assess the safety issues but allowed construction to proceed in the interim. The Province also refused to share the reports with First Nations or the public. Six months later, the BC government announced it had determined, based on the expert reports, that the proposed solutions were adequate and that it intended to move ahead with the project. The announcement did not address the impacts on Treaty 8 territory or the fact that significant legal challenges remain outstanding. It also did little to resolve First Nations' safety concerns, particularly given BC's refusal to share the reports until after the decision was issued.

Why It Matters

The Crown's ongoing failure to honourably implement treaties is one of the most critical barriers to achieving reconciliation with Indigenous Peoples. The Indigenous signatories to Treaty 8 entered into the treaty to establish a relationship of mutual respect, benefit and peaceful coexistence with incoming settlers. In exchange, the Crown promised, among other things, that the Indigenous treaty parties would be as free to hunt and fish after the treaty as if they had never entered into it.

The permanent destruction of significant portions of Treaty 8 is antithetical to this promise. BC's decision to forge ahead with the Site C project, even when both treaty rights and public safety are at stake, is further testament to how treaty rights can be undermined when the entity that determines whether a project goes ahead—the provincial government—also has a vested interest in the project proceeding.

Looking ahead

The Site C announcement marked the latest in a series of recent decisions by the BC government that call into question the Province's stated commitments to reconciliation. It also caps off one hundred fifty years of decision-making based on policies fundamentally rooted in racist assumptions about Indigenous Peoples. However, BC's failure to honour its treaty obligations does not mean Site C will proceed.

First, courts have confirmed the importance of implementing treaties in a way that respects and protects the Indigenous treaty parties' rights and territories, including by taking into account the cumulative effects of resource development and justifying any infringement of the treaty. The BC Supreme Court will determine whether the Province has met these obligations in West Moberly First Nations' treaty infringement action, which is scheduled to be heard over one hundred twenty days beginning in March 2022.

In addition, there are signs the Province's announcement will serve to strengthen First Nations' commitment to work together in Alberta and BC to ensure their rights are respected. In February, the Treaty 8 First Nations of Alberta issued a "Declaration of Indigenous Solidarity" calling for the immediate suspension of the Site C project until the Crown's consultation obligations are fulfilled and the court has determined West Moberly's treaty infringement claim.

In light of the growing opposition and uncertainty surrounding Site C, BC would be well-advised to reconsider whether a project that jeopardizes treaty rights and the safety of First Nation communities is truly in the public interest. Just as importantly, the Province should consider whether it is worth proceeding with a project that would perpetuate its decades-long policy of disregarding Indigenous rights and lands in order to advance its own economic and political interests.

Why Quebec but Not Indigenous Appointments to the Supreme Court?

The Supreme Court of Canada's Reference re Supreme Court Act decision in 2014 nullifying the appointment of Justice Nadon to the court is of importance to Indigenous people seeking justice through the Canadian court system.

Since 1875 there has been a requirement that a certain number of seats on the Supreme Court be reserved for Quebec. There is no equivalent requirement that any seats on the court be reserved for Indigenous people.

The majority of the Supreme Court in the Nadon decision concluded that Justice Nadon was ineligible for one of the Quebec seats because at the time of his appointment he was not a member of the Quebec bench or the Quebec bar.

Importantly, the court held that one of the purposes for Quebec seats on the court was to "ensure that Quebec's distinct legal traditions and social values are represented on the court, thereby enhancing the confidence of the people of Quebec in the Supreme Court as the final arbiter of their rights."

The court's reasoning in the Nadon decision lends support to calls for Indigenous appointments to the Supreme Court. The composition of the Supreme Court rightly recognizes

Quebec's special place in confederation. There is no historical, legal or principled justification for not also recognizing
the special place of Indigenous people.

Respect for the distinct legal traditions and social values of
Indigenous people has been enshrined through section 35 of
the constitution. Persistent government denial of Indigenous
rights has forced Indigenous people into the Canadian court
system in search of justice with the Supreme Court as the
final arbiter of their rights. To enhance Indigenous people's
confidence in the Canadian legal system and to ensure the
recognition of the distinct legal traditions and social values
of Indigenous people, qualified Indigenous people should be
appointed to the Supreme Court.

This issue remains an important subject of national
debate, especially amid the revitalization of Indigenous legal
orders across the country and courts' increasing engagement
with Indigenous law in their judgments. Unfortunately, the
federal government has not lived up to its lofty rhetoric. It
has continued to bypass qualified Indigenous candidates for
the Supreme Court based on the flimsy excuse that they have
not done their time as members of lower courts, ignoring
the fact that non-Indigenous people have been appointed
to the court without previous experience as judges. It has
also exhibited a willingness to perpetuate systemic racism
by insisting that qualified Indigenous candidates for the
Supreme Court be "bilingual"—i.e., fluent in both English
and French. The welcomed appointment of Mary Simon as
Governor General underlines the federal government's hyp-
ocrisy. Simon does not speak French. Any attempt to square
Simon's appointment as Governor General with the French

language requirement for the Supreme Court is a peculiar
Canadian exercise in cognitive dissonance.

Reconciliation as a Massive Failure

Anishinaabe comedian Ryan McMahon is one of Canada's most perceptive social commentators. Season five of McMahon's *Red Man Laughing* podcast is devoted to reconciliation. In his view, the brand of reconciliation peddled by Canada's mainstream politicians is a massive failure. For many lawyers, McMahon's critique likely grates on their ears. For those willing to be nudged out of their comfort zone, McMahon's criticism rings true.

Reconciliation continues to fail because it rests on a foundation of systemic racism. It is predicated on the denial of Indigenous Peoples' inherent rights and the willingness of the Canadian state to use violence to suppress Indigenous rights.

Reconciliation continues to fail because it attempts the impossible—the reconciliation of a right with a lie. The right is the pre-existing interest Indigenous Peoples had and continue to have in their land and the right to make decisions about their land before and after the colonizers' arrival. This includes the right to benefit from their land and decide how their lands should be used or not used.

The lie is that through simply showing up and planting a flag, European nations could acquire an interest in Indigenous land and displace Indigenous laws.

Around the world, this racist legal principle is recognized as the Doctrine of Discovery. It was developed by the United States Supreme Court in the 1830s. In the Supreme Court of Canada's 1990 *Sparrow* decision, where the court articulated for the first time the fundamental principles for interpreting section 35 of the constitution, it was welcomed as an essential principle of Canadian law.

While the Doctrine of Discovery was codified as part of Canadian law in the 1990s, its rationale was nothing new for Indigenous Peoples—by then it had become all too familiar to them. For decades and generations they had been faced with the denial of their laws, of their title to the land, of the true spirit and intent of treaties, of their very humanity.

Denial is the handmaiden of violence. When grainy images hover on TVs and computer screens of Indigenous Peoples assaulted by agents of the Canadian state, the legacy and modern reality of denial upsets smug complacency. In that discomfort the opportunity for real reconciliation is born.

Confronted with the reality that rote, feel-good land acknowledgements are part of the problem, not the solution, Canadians will hopefully start to demand deliverables. What are the courts and mainstream politicians doing to undo hundreds of years of violence and denial? What is being done to ensure that Indigenous laws are respected, that Indigenous Peoples benefit from their lands and are actively involved in deciding how their lands are used?

As hard as it might be for Canadians to hear McMahon's condemnation of reconciliation as it is currently practised, his criticism is also an invitation. It is an invitation to Canadians to take the first step on what will undoubtedly be a long and difficult road.

The first step is acceptance. Acceptance that Canada is fundamentally a racist state. That it has been built on the denial of Indigenous Peoples' rights and humanity. That this denial is a shameful fact that runs through and binds together Canadian law.

With acceptance comes opportunity.

The Case for Denying Indigenous Rights

Denial is cumulative.

It has a beginning. At a certain time in a certain place a decision is made to ignore someone else's existing rights. There's resistance. The true rights holders fight back. But advantage is taken. Protest is suppressed. Wealth and power grow. For the dominant society, as denials accumulate injustice fades from sight. The status quo emerges. Calls for justice are denigrated and ridiculed.

Resistance persists.

Prodded by the children of those who witnessed denial at its conception, the courts assume the role of archaeologists. Layer upon layer of indignity is scraped away. The underlying lie is revealed.

A choice emerges.

Acknowledge the original wrong, apologize and commit to making amends or double down on denial. As the excavation work continues and politicians slowly respond to the colonizing society's unease with the basis for its comfort and privilege, denial's voice becomes increasingly apocalyptic.

Writing in the *Globe and Mail*, Tom Flanagan, a former Harper advisor, declared that the new Liberal federal government's intention to implement the United Nations

Declaration on the Rights of Indigenous Peoples (UNDRIP) has "great potential for mischief..."

According to Flanagan, recognizing the UNDRIP principle of free, prior and informed consent is a recipe for economic ruin because Indigenous land rights in Canada are poorly defined, some Indigenous people might consider consent to be a veto and because without the threat of expropriation Canadian governments will have a hard time building long-distance corridor projects (e.g., pipelines, railways, highways and power lines).

Flanagan's message is clear: implementing UNDRIP is dangerous because it is contrary to Canada's and the provinces' long-established policy of denying Aboriginal title, rights and treaty rights.

The Fraser Institute, which describes itself as communicating the effects of government policies and entrepreneurship on the well-being of Canadians and is described by others as a propaganda outfit for "well-fed libertarians, conservatives and reactionaries," has also warned of economic disaster on the horizon.

In a report ominously entitled "Economic Development in Jeopardy?" it warns that the 2015 *Saik'uz* decision from the British Columbia Court of Appeal threatened to open the door for Aboriginal title litigation against private companies.

The report's primary complaint was that the court's decision extends to First Nations the same legal right that has always been enjoyed by corporations and non-Indigenous people: they can sue others based on an alleged interest in land but have to prove the interest as part of the trial.

Denial's argument is simple.

Having based a national economy on the oppression of Indigenous Peoples' legal rights, the consequences of changing course are potentially catastrophic. Better to damn the torpedoes and count on the resurgence of the denial agenda. Or, at the very least, work to impede the re-establishment of Indigenous rights and jurisdiction until the dams and pipelines are built, the oil extracted, and the rivers and lakes destroyed.

The case for denying Indigenous rights rests on colonialism's inertia. Its strength is fear and self-interest. Its weakness is a growing awareness that while Canada preaches the rule of law, justice and fairness abroad, the country's wealth and privilege originates with an overarching historic wrong.

Denial has a beginning. Hopefully, it also has an end.

A Cold Rain Falls: Canada's Proposed UNDRIP Legislation

After years of false starts, the federal government has taken a tentative step toward implementing the United Nations Declaration on the Rights of Indigenous Peoples by introducing Bill C-15. Is this really a game changer for Indigenous Peoples in Canada? I have my doubts, as do others.

There are two main reasons for skepticism. First, Bill C-15 focuses on high-level, aspirational commitments rather than on delivering concrete, immediate change to Indigenous Peoples. If passed into law, Bill C-15 will require the federal government to take measures to ensure the laws of Canada are consistent with the declaration, and to prepare and implement an action plan to achieve the objectives of the declaration. While enacting sweeping changes to federal legislation will undoubtedly take time, the federal government's focus on these future promises conveniently allows it to sidestep the realities that Indigenous people face on a daily basis.

Governments pour promises on Indigenous people like a winter rain. Rather than witnessing real change, we are too often left with cold disappointment. Maybe it'll be different this time. But, if the experience of British Columbia's UNDRIP legislation is an accurate predictor, we should all dress accordingly.

Passed a little over a year ago to great fanfare, the BC Declaration on the Rights of Indigenous Peoples Act has failed to live up to its promise. Instead, the provincial government has continued with its dreary, self-serving narrative based on the denial of Indigenous rights. The provincial government's business-as-usual approach to recognizing and protecting Indigenous rights is a choice of its own making. Rather than interpreting the UNDRIP law as being immediately actionable, the provincial government has interpreted it as being merely aspirational and forward-looking.

A case in point was the provincial government's abysmal response in early 2020 to attempts by the Wet'suwet'en to protect their land and waters from the Coastal GasLink pipeline. Rather than using new legislation as a tool to resolve conflict in a way that respects Indigenous rights and law, the provincial government chose to disregard its own law. All indicators are that the federal government intends to take a similar approach—lofty promises followed by a continuation of the grim reality of denial and oppression. If so, rather than delivering results, Bill C-15 will sow further cynicism.

The second, and more fundamental, reason for skepticism about Canada's UNDRIP bill is that the lack of respect for Indigenous rights in Canada is not due to a shortage of legal obligations—it is the federal and provincial governments' refusal to fulfill those obligations.

From the Royal Proclamation of 1763 to the current federal government's refusal to implement the Supreme Court's *Marshall* decision on the Mi'kmaw commercial fishing right, the federal and provincial governments' legal obligations have been clear. What has been and continues to be lacking is a commitment by Canadian governments to follow the law, followed by demonstrable action.

On this point it is important to emphasize that Indigenous rights in Canada are not dependent on implementing UNDRIP—these rights exist both as inherent rights and rights protected under section 35 of the constitution. The point of the UNDRIP legislation is not to create Indigenous rights, but rather to hold the federal government to the international legal standards it has publicly endorsed. Given Canada's long history of failing to live up to its own well-established and clear domestic legal standards, why should Indigenous people expect the federal government to suddenly change colours when it comes to respecting international law?

Rather than a new day of respect for and recognition of Indigenous rights in Canada, the passage of Bill C-15 will most likely mark the beginning of a fresh round of efforts, legal and political, by Indigenous people to force the federal government to live up to its commitments.

The measure for real change is concrete, on-the-ground implementation and respect for Indigenous Peoples' inherent and constitutional rights—not another set of commitments to do something in the future.

Maybe I'm wrong. Maybe the passage of Bill C-15 will peel back the clouds and the sun will shine. Personally, I'm not putting away my raincoat just yet.

Colonialism's Disciples: How Government Undermines Indigenous People

There are a lot of well-intentioned civil servants. They respect Indigenous people and do their best, within the confines of their positions, to bend government policy to achieve just outcomes. Their work is recognized, appreciated and honoured. This essay is not about them.

This is about government employees, federal and provincial, who spend their workdays undermining Indigenous Peoples.

Case in point. On a winter's day I drove the Trans-Canada highway from Winnipeg to Kenora. It's a car journey loaded with memories, contradictions and hope.

As an undergraduate I spent a summer camped on a small island in Shoal Lake while soil sampling for a junior mining company. Now I represent Shoal Lake 40 First Nation. Close to the Ontario border I pass the Freedom Road sign, Shoal Lake 40's statement of defiance and optimism for the future.

Having managed to keep the car on the road for two plus hours despite not being able to get a rental with winter tires at the Winnipeg airport, I check in at the Lakeside Inn close to midnight.

Dawn finds me giving thanks for the view of Lake of the Woods from the hotel's ninth-floor restaurant. Boats, cornered by the ice, sit motionless, patiently waiting for the sun to regain its strength and set them free.

While I drink coffee and prepare for a meeting with Treaty 3 clients and government officials, a group of four or five settle around the table behind me. There are few people in the restaurant and I can't help but overhear their conversation.

I realize they work for one of those government departments which, despite regular name changes, always has an acronym that sticks in your throat. They are the government employees my clients and I will meet after breakfast.

They too are preparing for the meeting. My first thought is to turn and introduce myself. But then their words settle in my consciousness. They are rehearsing the various ways they intend to say no to my clients.

They are also laughing. Laughing at their own well-worn obstructionist tactics. Laughing at my clients' positions and expectations. Laughing at the ultimate meaninglessness of the consultation process they have invited my clients to join.

My hand drifts across the notepad and I find myself scribbling in the margin:

The beetles gathered, stuffing their ears with indifference,
stabbing their eyes, filling their mouths with silence.

My experience at the Lakeside Inn was extreme but not exceptional. It wasn't the first time I've overheard government employees laughing about how they plan to stonewall Indigenous people.

I also believe it is not representative of the majority of civil servants who honestly want to make a positive difference. But it is significant nonetheless, especially when governments pledge a renewed partnership with Indigenous Peoples.

The Supreme Court of Canada has penned inspiring descriptions of the purpose and importance of the Crown's obligations under section 35 of the constitution. With varying degrees of sincerity, governments have echoed the court's pronouncements.

Cynicism grinds legal principles and government mandates to dust.

However small a group they might be, government employees who walk in colonialism's shadow do a disservice to us all.

They undermine the legal and historical relationship between Canada and Indigenous Peoples. They thwart government policy. They make a mockery of the law.

Most importantly, they crush the good faith and optimism of Indigenous people who enter into consultation processes with the hope that government is finally serious about a partnership based on respect.

Legal principles, government promises and cabinet appointments are important. But until Indigenous people are confident that the bureaucrats they meet on a daily basis sincerely believe that their responsibility is to work with, not against, Indigenous people, none of us will be free of Canada's colonial past.

Made of Sterner Stuff—The Problem with Allies

Allies depress me more than opponents.

Many who outright disagree with me about respecting Indigenous rights are open to persuasion. I don't include the committed racists in this category. I'm talking about those whose opinions rest on a lack of information, context and empathy. If I listen to them honestly and without judgement, they often do the same for me. When they realize I will not ridicule them for their opinions, they become more receptive. They begin to acknowledge I might have a point—maybe they should have a rethink.

For example, several years ago I spoke to a group of people working in a resource extraction industry. As expected, I didn't receive a warm reception. For an hour and a half I fielded questions and comments I hear on a regular basis: *Why can't we all be treated equally? Indians don't pay taxes. Don't your clients want to work?*

After explaining that my clients do in fact pay taxes, that they are the hardest-working people I know and why all Canadians should be proud the constitution protects collective rights, many (but not all) in the audience began to reconsider their received opinions. By the end of the session their hostility had been replaced by friendliness and a greater understanding of the legal and historical context for recognizing Indigenous rights. I left the session exhausted and hopeful.

In contrast, allies can move me to tears. I'm not referring to the vast majority who are well intentioned and committed to doing their best to understand a complex issue and play a supportive role. I'm not even referring to the minority who indulge in "performative allyship"—they are easily recognizable and increasingly find themselves without an audience.

The people I have in mind are the handful of allies perfectly suited to be cast as judges in a game show entitled *Defend Your Life*. Usually well-educated and comfortably white, buoyed and insulated by entitlement and privilege, they rush forward with opinions, criticisms and superior insights unburdened by doubt or humility.

I often encounter these people when my criticism touches their core understanding of what it means to be Canadian. On the second anniversary of the acquittal of the Saskatchewan farmer who killed Colten Boushie, I gave a talk to a group of allies about the systemic violence perpetrated against Indigenous people by non-Indigenous Canadians and the Canadian state (my talk was based on "Reconciliation at the End of Gun" on page 138). It was a difficult talk to give. Professionally, we had just witnessed the RCMP's arrest of our Wet'suwet'en clients. Personally, it stirred memories of growing up in rural Manitoba.

At the end of my talk, an ally rushed forward to challenge me. The nub of his rebuttal was "Indians killed Indians before white men arrived." Looking around the room I noticed one of Colten's cousins eager to speak to me but blocked by this domineering ally. I struggled to distance myself from him and to contain my emotions. I was being corrected, put in my place by a white man confident not just in his opinions but in his right and, from his perspective, his obligation to school me.

I felt myself back in grade school, a kid without privilege, confident in my family's support but constantly reminded of my position on the margins of respectability. At some point in high school, I realized that questioning had limits. A line existed between acceptable, polite criticism and the unspeakable. The national myth of "Canada the good" was sacrosanct. Cross the line and you risked being disciplined, punished, cast out.

Some allies do more than act as self-appointed arbiters of acceptable discourse; they strive to establish themselves as stronger and more determined than those they purport to support.

Two days after news emerged of the bodies of 215 Indigenous children discovered at the Kamloops Indian Residential School, I was about to sit down for dinner with my family. Knowing that clients, friends and family members across the country were struggling with loss and grief, I was engulfed in a fog of sadness and despair.

Unthinkingly, I opened the email on my phone. Waiting for me was an email in reply to an essay I had published nine months earlier ("Reconciliation as a Massive Failure," on page 168). The writer was a self-described member of a well-known national non-profit organization dedicated to dismantling racism and colonization. The tragic news from Kamloops had motivated him to reach out to me. He had a problem with my use of the word *acceptance* in the second to last paragraph of my essay, when I wrote, "The first step is acceptance. Acceptance that Canada is fundamentally a racist state." In his view I should have used *acknowledge* because the word is "made of sterner stuff." For my edification, he helpfully included dictionary definitions.

I had never cried in front of my kids. But in that moment, slumped over the table with my head in my hands, I cried. I cried for the 215 children and their families. I cried for all the stolen, abused and murdered Indigenous children across Canada. I cried for my lack of words to explain any of this to my children. I cried for the marginalized, oppressed and abused whose voices are stolen and silenced by their allies.

How the Canadian Legal System Fails Indigenous People

Clinging to the program
Obviously
Is the obvious lie
The past is more than a memory
—John Trudell, "What It Means to Be a Human Being" (2001)

Law school is the great revealer. It reveals motivation: greed, social justice, couldn't get into medical school. It reveals ignorance.

Case in point. Sitting in a law school lecture theatre. A law professor is making an earnest effort to convince skeptical students it's important for future lawyers to know at least a little about the history of the Canadian state's relationship with Indigenous Peoples. In the front of the room a hand shoots up.

"Yes, do you have a question?"

"Didn't the Indians kill all the buffalo?"

Years later. On my feet in a courtroom. Facing judges with skeptical faces as I give a quick overview of *Badger*, *Haida Nation* and *Mikisew* to explain how treaties between the Crown and Indigenous Peoples give rise to a constitutional obligation to consult and accommodate.

A voice from the front interrupts me.

"Mr. McIvor, this treaty you're talking about, is it part of a statute?"

I'm seldom at a loss for words in court. As every litigator knows, when the moment comes to speak the words tumble out, origin unknown, forming themselves into sentences of varying degrees of coherence.

Not this time. This time I paused. For the judges I faced, and for the government and industry lawyers staring at the back of my head, the pause was likely too short to notice. For me it spanned generations.

Ignorance is not an absence. Ignorance is a force. It justifies. It silences. It perpetuates.

University students become law students. Law students become lawyers. Lawyers become judges. Judges decide.

Judges decide where the boundaries are. The boundaries between the Canada that was and the Canada that will be. To assume they can do their job without a basic understanding of Canadian colonialism and Aboriginal law is more than a failure to appreciate the relationship between knowledge, understanding and justice.

It is to willfully enlist the power of ignorance in an unacknowledged campaign to deny Indigenous Peoples their past, present and future.

Lakehead University and the University of Winnipeg have mandated that every student take at least one Indigenous studies course. The Truth and Reconciliation Commission recommends that lawyers receive appropriate cultural competency training, including the history of treaties and Aboriginal rights and that Canadian law schools require students to take a course in Indigenous Peoples and the law which would also include the history of treaties and Aboriginal rights.

These are important steps toward subduing the power of ignorance. Without these and other policies that ensure lawyers and judges are educated about Indigenous Peoples, history and the law, the Canadian legal system will continue to fail Indigenous Peoples.

The past is more than a memory. It can oppress. It can light the way. The choice is ours.

Further Reading

Looking to learn more about Indigenous rights? I hope you find this reading list informative and helpful. It is not meant to be exhaustive.

Aboriginal and Treaty Rights

Asch, Michael, *On Being Here to Stay: Treaties and Aboriginal Rights in Canada* (University of Toronto Press, 2014).

Borrows, John & Michael Coyle, eds., *The Right Relationship: Reimagining the Implementation of Historical Treaties* (University of Toronto Press, 2017).

Chartrand, Paul L.A.H., ed., *Who Are Canada's Aboriginal Peoples?: Recognition, Definition, and Jurisdiction* (Purich Publishing, 2002).

Christie, Gordon, *Canadian Law and Indigenous Self-Determination: A Naturalist Analysis* (University of Toronto Press, 2019).

Foster, Hamar, Heather Raven & Jeremy Webber, eds., *Let Right Be Done: Aboriginal Title, the Calder Case and the Future of Indigenous Rights* (UBC Press, 2007).

Hoehn, Felix, *Reconciling Sovereignties: Aboriginal Nations and Canada* (University of Saskatchewan Native Law Centre, 2012).

Johnson, Harold, *Two Families: Treaties and Government*
(Purich Publishing, 2007).

McNeil, Kent, *Flawed Precedent: The* St. Catherine's *Case and
Aboriginal Title* (UBC Press, 2019).

Nichols, Joshua, *A Reconciliation without Recollection?: An
Investigation of the Foundations of Aboriginal Law in Canada*
(University of Toronto Press, 2019).

Reynolds, Jim, *Aboriginal Peoples and the Law: A Critical
Introduction* (UBC Press, 2018).

Reynolds, Jim, *From Wardship to Rights: The* Guerin *Case and
Aboriginal Law* (UBC Press, 2020).

Indigenous Law

Borrows, John, *Canada's Indigenous Constitution* (University of
Toronto Press, 2010).

Borrows, John, *Freedom and Indigenous Constitutionalism*
(University of Toronto Press, 2016).

Cameron, Angela, Sari Graben & Val Napoleon, eds., *Creating
Indigenous Property: Power, Rights, and Relationships*
(University of Toronto Press, 2020).

Craft, Aimée, *Breathing Life into the Stone Fort Treaty: An
Anishnabe Understanding of Treaty One* (Purich Publishing,
2013).

Friedland, Hadley Louise, *The* Wetiko *Legal Principles: Cree
and Anishinabek Responses to Violence and Victimization*
(University of Toronto Press, 2018).

McAdam, Sylvia (Saysewahum), *Nationhood Interrupted:
Revitalizing nêhiyaw Legal Systems* (Purich Publishing,
2015).

University of Victoria Indigenous Law Research Unit,
*Mikomosis and the Wetiko: A Teaching Guide for Youth,
Community, and Post-Secondary Educators* (University of
Victoria Indigenous Law Research Unit, 2013).

International, Indigenous and Canadian Law

Borrows, John, Larry Chartrand, Oonagh E. Fitzgerald &
Risa Schwartz, eds., *Braiding Legal Orders: Implementing
the United Nations Declaration on the Rights of Indigenous
Peoples* (McGill-Queen's University Press, 2019).
Drake, Karen & Brenda L. Gunn, eds., *Renewing Relationships:
Indigenous Peoples and Canada* (University of Saskatchewan
Native Law Centre, 2019).
Hartley, Jackie, Paul Joffe & Jennifer Preston, eds., *Realizing the
UN Declaration on the Rights of Indigenous Peoples: Triumph,
Hope, and Action* (UBC Press, 2010).
Lightfoot, Sheryl, *Global Indigenous Politics: A Subtle Revolution*
(Routledge, 2016).
Morales, Sarah & Joshua Nichols, "Reconciliation Beyond the
Box: The UN Declaration and Plurinational Federalism in
Canada" (Centre for International Governance Innovation,
2018).

Aboriginal Law Case Summaries and Commentary

Borrows, John & Leonard Rotman, *Aboriginal Legal Issues:
Cases, Materials and Commentary*, 5th edition (LexisNexis,
2018).

Decembrini, Angela D'Elia, Kate Gunn, Bruce McIvor & Shin
Imai, *Annotated Aboriginal Law 2021: The Constitution,
Legislation, Treaties and Supreme Court of Canada Case
Summaries* (Thomson Reuters, 2020).

Rudin, Jonathan, *Indigenous People and the Criminal Justice
System: A Practitioner's Handbook* (Emond Publishing, 2018).

Commissions and Inquiries

*Final Report of the National Inquiry into Missing and Murdered
Indigenous Women and Girls* (2019).

*Final Report of the Truth and Reconciliation Commission of
Canada, Volume One, Summary: Honouring the Truth,
Reconciling for the Future* (2015).

Report of the Royal Commission on Aboriginal Peoples (1996).

Indigenous Resurgence and Reconciliation

Adams, Howard, *Prison of Grass: Canada from a Native Point of
View*, 2nd edition (Fifth House Books, 1989).

Akiwenzie-Damm, Kateri, et al., *This Place: 150 Years Retold*
(HighWater Press, 2019).

Alfred, Taiaiake, *Wasáse: Indigenous Pathways of Action and
Freedom* (University of Toronto Press, 2005).

Asch, Michael, John Borrows & James Tully, eds., *Resurgence
and Reconciliation: Indigenous-Settler Relations and Earth
Teachings* (University of Toronto Press, 2018).

Campbell, Maria, *Halfbreed* (Random House of Canada, 2019).

Cardinal, Harold, *The Unjust Society: The Tragedy of Canada's
Indians*, 2nd edition (Douglas & McIntyre, 1999).

Coburn, Elaine, ed., *More Will Sing Their Way to Freedom: Indigenous Resistance and Resurgence* (Fernwood Publishing, 2015).

Coulthard, Glen Sean, *Red Skin, White Masks: Rejecting the Colonial Politics of Recognition* (University of Minnesota Press, 2014).

Green, Joyce, ed., *Making Space for Indigenous Feminism* (Fernwood Publishing, 2017).

Hill, Gord & Ward Churchill, *The 500 Years of Resistance Comic Book* (Arsenal Pulp Press, 2002).

Joseph, Bob, *21 Things You May Not Know About the Indian Act: Helping Canadians Make Reconciliation with Indigenous Peoples a Reality* (Indigenous Relations Press, 2018).

King, Thomas, *The Inconvenient Indian: A Curious Account of Native People in North America* (Random House of Canada, 2013).

Kino-nda-niimi Collective, ed., *The Winter We Danced: Voices from the Past, the Future, and the Idle No More Movement* (ARP Books, 2014).

Manuel, Arthur, *Unsettling Canada: A National Wake-Up Call* (Between the Lines, 2015).

Manuel, Arthur & Grand Chief Ronald Derrickson, *The Reconciliation Manifesto: Recovering the Land, Rebuilding the Economy* (Lorimer, 2017).

Manuel, George & Michael Posluns, *The Fourth World: An Indian Reality* (University of Minnesota Press, 2019).

Maracle, Lee, *I Am Woman: A Native Perspective on Sociology and Feminism* (Press Gang, 2003).

Maracle, Lee, *Bobbi Lee Indian Rebel*, 2nd edition (Women's Press, 2017).

McFarlane, Peter & Nicole Schabus, eds. *Whose Land Is It Anyway?: A Manual for Decolonization* (Federation of Post-Secondary Educators of BC, 2017).

Monture-Angus, Patricia, *Thunder in My Soul: A Mohawk Woman Speaks* (Brunswick Books, 1995).

Palmater, Pamela, *Indigenous Nationhood: Empowering Grassroots Citizens* (Fernwood Publishing, 2015).

Saul, John Ralston, *The Comeback: How Aboriginals Are Reclaiming Power and Influence* (Penguin Canada, 2015).

Sellars, Bev, *Price Paid: The Fight for First Nations Survival* (Talonbooks, 2016).

Simpson, Audra, *Mohawk Interruptus: Political Life Across the Borders of Settler States* (Duke University Press, 2014).

Simpson, Leanne Betasamosake, *Dancing on Our Turtle's Back: Stories of Nishnaabeg Re-Creation, Resurgence, and a New Emergence* (ARP Books, 2011).

Simpson, Leanne Betasamosake, *As We Have Always Done: Indigenous Freedom Through Radical Resistance* (University of Minnesota Press, 2017).

Settler Colonial Law and Decolonization

Bhandar, Brenna, *Colonial Lives of Property: Law, Land, and Racial Regimes of Ownership* (Duke University Press, 2018).

Chartrand, Paul L.A.H., *Manitoba's Metis Settlement Scheme of 1870* (University of Saskatchewan Native Law Centre, 1991).

Crosby, Andrew & Jeffrey Monaghan, *Policing Indigenous Movements: Dissent and the Security State* (Fernwood Publishing, 2018).

Daschuk, James, *Clearing the Plains: Disease, Politics of Starvation, and the Loss of Aboriginal Life* (University of Regina Press, 2013).

Davis, Lynne, ed., *Alliances: Re/Envisioning Indigenous-non-Indigenous Relationships* (University of Toronto Press, 2010).

Johnson, Harold, *Peace and Good Order: The Case for Indigenous Justice in Canada* (Random House of Canada, 2019).

Kelm, Mary-Ellen & Keith D. Smith, *Talking Back to the Indian Act: Critical Readings in Settler Colonial Histories* (University of Toronto Press, 2018).

Lowman, Emma Battell & Adam J. Barker, *Settler: Identity and Colonialism in 21st Century Canada* (Fernwood Publishing, 2015).

Mackey, Eva, *Unsettled Expectations: Uncertainty, Land, and Settler Decolonization* (Fernwood Publishing, 2016).

Morgensen, Scott Lauria, *Spaces Between Us: Queer Settler Colonialism and Indigenous Decolonization* (University of Minnesota Press, 2011).

Regan, Paulette, *Unsettling the Settler Within: Indian Residential Schools, Truth Telling, and Reconciliation in Canada* (UBC Press, 2011).

Robertson, Lindsay G., *Conquest by Law: How the Discovery of America Dispossessed Indigenous Peoples of their Lands* (Oxford University Press, 2007).

Teillet, Jean, *The North-West Is Our Mother: The Story of Louis Riel's People, the Métis Nation* (Harper Collins Canada, 2019).

Index I: General

Index II: Court Decisions

PHOTO CREDIT: KATHRYN LANGSFORD

About the Author

Dr. Bruce McIvor is recognized nationally and internationally as one of Canada's leading lawyers in Aboriginal law. Bruce represents First Nations across Canada and teaches at the University of British Columbia's Allard School of Law. His great-grandparents took Métis scrip at Red River in Manitoba. He is a member of the Manitoba Métis Federation.